Teacher's Guide

Reading EXPLORER

1

Nancy Douglas • Nancy Hubley

HEINLE
CENGAGE Learning™

Australia • Brazil • Japan • Korea • Mexico • Singapore • Spain • United Kingdom • United States

HEINLE
CENGAGE Learning™

Reading Explorer Teacher's Guide 1
Nancy Douglas and Nancy Hubley

VP and Director of Operations:
Vincent Grosso

Publisher: Andrew Robinson

Executive Editor: Sean Bermingham

Senior Development Editor: Derek Mackrell

Assistant Editor: Claire Tan

Director of Global Marketing: Ian Martin

Director of US Marketing: Jim McDonough

Content Project Manager: Tan Jin Hock

Senior Print Buyer: Mary Beth Hennebury

National Geographic Coordinator:
Leila Hishmeh

Contributing Editor: Joan Ho

Cover Designer: Page 2, LLC

Compositor: Pre-PressPMG

Acknowledgments
The Author and Publishers would like to thank
the following teaching professionals for their
valuable feedback during the development of
this series.

Jamie Ahn, English Coach, Seoul;
Heidi Bundschoks, ITESM, Sinaloa México;
José Olavo de Amorim, Colégio Bandeirantes,
São Paulo; **Marina Gonzalez**, Instituto
Universitario de Lenguas Modernas Pte.,
Buenos Aires; **Tsung-Yuan Hsiao**, National
Taiwan Ocean University, Keelung; **Michael
Johnson**, Muroran Institute of Technology;
Thays Ladosky, Colégio Damas, Recife; **Ahmed
Mohamed Motala**, University of Sharjah;
David Persey, British Council, Bangkok;
David Schneer, ACS International, Singapore;
Atsuko Takase, Kinki University, Osaka;
Deborah E. Wilson, American University
of Sharjah

This series is dedicated to the memory of Joe
Dougherty, who was a constant inspiration
throughout its development.

For permission to use material from this text or product,
submit all requests online at **www.cengage.com/permissions**
Further permissions questions can be emailed to
permissionrequest@cengage.com

ISBN-13: 978-1-4240-2889-4

ISBN-10: 1-4240-2889-2

US edition ISBN-13: 978-1-4240-4551-8

US edition ISBN-10: 1-4240-4551-7

Heinle
20 Channel Center Street
Boston, Massachusetts 02210
USA

Cengage Learning is a leading provider of customized learning solutions with
office locations around the globe, including Singapore, the United Kingdom,
Australia, Mexico, Brazil, and Japan. Locate our local office at:
international.cengage.com/region

Cengage Learning products are represented in Canada by
Nelson Education, Ltd.

Visit Heinle online at **elt.heinle.com**

Visit our corporate website at **www.cengage.com**

Printed in the United States of America
1 2 3 4 5 6 7 – 13 12 11 10 09

Contents

Take a Tour of *Reading Explorer*

Thank you for choosing to use Reading Explorer Book 1. Here are 12 steps to help you get familiar with the course:

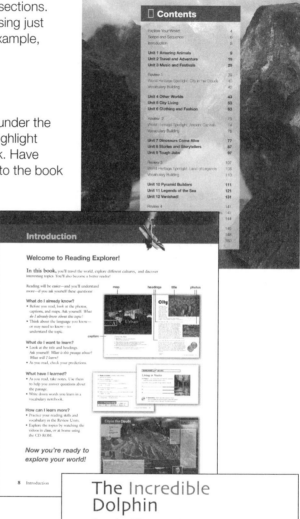

1. First, look at the list of **Contents** on page 3 of the Student Book. You'll see the book is organized into 12 units and 4 review sections. The book can be used for a short course of 24–36 hours using just the core units or can be extended for longer courses, for example, by using the video activities and review units in class.

2. Turn to the world map on pages 4–5 of the Student Book, under the title **Explore Your World!** The photographs and captions highlight some of the topics and places that are explored in the book. Have learners follow the page references as a way to get them into the book at the start of the first lesson.

3. Look at the **Scope and Sequence** on pages 6–7 of the Student Book. You'll see that each unit is based on a theme of general interest, for example, "Amazing Animals." Within each unit are two lessons, each based around a reading passage. You'll also note the range of vocabulary building skills covered in the book.

4. Read the **Introduction** on page 8 of the Student Book. It explains a general approach to developing reading skills commonly known as *KWL*. The aim of this approach—and of this course, in general—is to develop active, fluent readers. For more on teaching reading skills, see pages 8–12 of this Teacher's Guide.

5. Skim through a **Unit** of the Student Book and compare it against the Unit Walkthrough on the following pages of this Teacher's Guide. Each unit is accompanied in the Teacher's Guide by teaching suggestions and background notes (see pages 18–73).

6. Turn to one of the **Reading Passages** in the Student Book (e.g., Student Book page 11). The reading passages are all adapted from authentic National Geographic sources, which are listed in the **Credits** on page 160 of the Student Book. Each reading passage is also available as an audio recording on the **Classroom Audio CD** as well as on the **Student CD-ROM**, providing a useful model for pronunciation and intonation.

7. You'll note in each reading passage that useful, high-frequency words are highlighted in red. These **Target Vocabulary** words are listed on pages 145–147 of the Student Book, and also, with definitions, at the back of this Teacher's Guide (pages 74–78). For suggestions on teaching vocabulary, see pages 12–14 of this Teacher's Guide.

8. Check out the **Video clips** on the Video DVD and Student CD-ROM. The clips can be used with the **Explore More** section at the end of each Student Book unit, and also with the video comprehension activities on the Student CD-ROM. The scripts for the videos are on pages 148–157 of the Student Book. You'll see that the video narration recycles many of the target vocabulary items. For ideas on using video in class, see pages 15–16 of this Teacher's Guide.

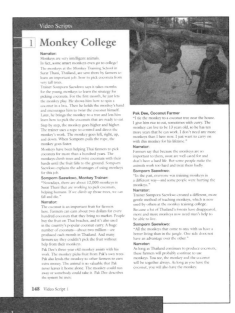

9. After each set of three units is a **Review** section (e.g., Student Book pages 39–42). Included in this section is a two-page **World Heritage Spotlight,** preceded by a **Field Notes** task. Suggestions for presenting these in class are provided in this Teacher's Guide (e.g., pages 30–31). The review units tie in with National Geographic Society's efforts to raise awareness of heritage and conservation.

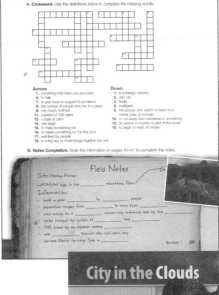

10. Check out the range of ancillary components of the course. The **Student CD-ROM** contains the 12 video clips, audio recordings of the 24 reading passages, and a variety of interactive comprehension and vocabulary activities. The activities are self-grading and provide reinforcement for the language presented in each unit. Additional learning and teaching resources are available online at elt.heinle.com/explorer.

11. An **Assessment CD-ROM** containing Exam*View*® question banks is available for teachers who want to create customized tests or give students additional language practice. See page 17 of this Teacher's Guide for suggestions on assessing learners' progress.

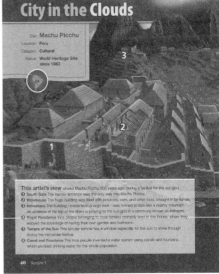

12. Finally, turn to the back page of this Teacher's Guide, and you'll see a list of recommended graded readers from the Heinle *Footprint Reading Library*, a range of nonfiction readers based on video content from National Geographic, and correlated with CEF (Common European Framework) levels. Extensive reading for pleasure is a proven way to promote reading proficiency. See elt.heinle.com/ng for the full range of leveled readers, audio, and video components.

Unit Walkthrough

Warm Up discussion questions help to raise learners' interest in the unit theme and activate learners' prior knowledge.

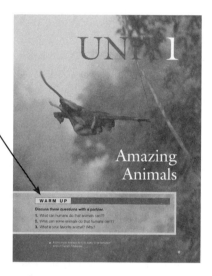

Before You Read tasks introduce key terms and content that learners will encounter in the reading passage, and develop previewing skills such as skimming and making predictions.

Each **Reading Passage** is adapted from an authentic National Geographic source; the language has been carefully graded and the reading contains ten high-frequency "target vocabulary" items.

Reading Comprehension tasks include a variety of graphic organizers, which help learners to understand the relationship between key ideas in the passage.

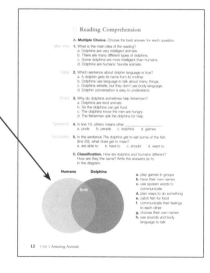

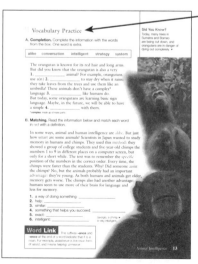

Vocabulary Practice activities reinforce the acquisition of "target vocabulary" items presented in the main passage.

6

A second reading in each unit expands learners' knowledge of the unit theme and further builds vocabulary.

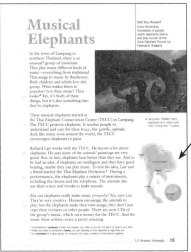

Maps, captions, charts, and graphs develop learners' visual literacy—their ability to decode graphic information effectively.

Reading Comprehension activities include question types commonly found in high-stakes international exams, such as TOEFL® and TOEIC®.

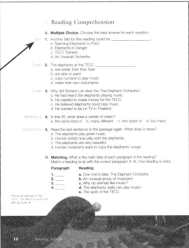

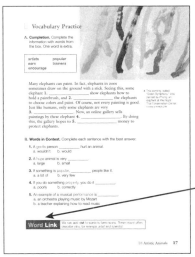

Vocabulary Builder boxes highlight common collocations, affixes, and usage to develop learner independence.

Explore More video activities provide additional comprehension and vocabulary practice while motivating learners to learn more about the unit topic.

Further comprehension and vocabulary practice is provided on the Student CD-ROM, which contains all 12 video clips, audio recordings of the 24 reading passages, and more than 80 self-scoring activities.

Aims and Principles of *Reading Explorer*

The *Reading Explorer* series aims to develop learners' skills in reading, vocabulary building, and critical thinking, using topics and visuals adapted from real-world National Geographic content.

A key principle of *Reading Explorer* is that today's learners need to be exposed to a wide variety of reading types. Information in the twenty-first century is increasingly conveyed in **multimodal** formats, that is, using a combination of text with graphics, diagrams, tables, photographs, and video. Exposure to the variety of formats in *Reading Explorer* will help learners to develop their visual literacy as well as textual literacy.

Another principle of *Reading Explorer* is that fluent readers employ a variety of strategies for reading, which, in turn, is based on various purposes for reading. In other words, the reading process is often **multipurpose**.

With *Reading Explorer*, learners develop strategies such as:

- Using their own background knowledge of the topic, and awareness of text types, in order to make predictions about a passage;
- Reading "top-down" to gain an overall idea of the purpose, type, and structure of a text;
- Processing "bottom-up" clues such as contextual information and word parts in order to comprehend unfamiliar vocabulary, and the meaning of cohesive markers such as pronoun references;
- Scanning a text quickly to locate specific information;
- Processing what is literally given in a text (literal comprehension) as well as what is implied or inferred by the writer (inferential comprehension);
- Recognizing relationships within a paragraph, or across a text, such as identifying cause and effect relationships, or the links between main and supporting ideas; and
- Identifying what is factually true in a text, versus the writer's personal opinion.

An additional principle of the series is that reading is a **multistage** process. In particular, learners should be well prepared before they start to read a text and should later have an opportunity to reflect on what they have learned. This concept is summarized in the **Introduction** on page 8 of the Student Book that outlines a framework known as the *KWL technique*.

Using this approach, students identify:

- What they **know** about the topic (i.e., their prior knowledge, or *schema*)
- What they **want** to know (i.e., their purpose for reading)
- What they **learned** (i.e., their comprehension of the reading)

With *Reading Explorer*, learners are also encouraged to go beyond the passage—and develop learner independence—by exploring the topic using the DVD, the Student CD-ROM, and the review units, as well as by exploring the topics online.

Preparing Learners to Read

How should teachers prepare for a unit?

Teachers should go through the unit themselves before a class, making note of any questions students may have. The Teacher's Guide provides background information and resources to help deal with students' questions. Relevant websites provide opportunities to learn more, and students can be directed to them for further exploration. Take time to read the overview, answer keys, and detailed teaching notes on language, cultural background, and vocabulary. The **Explore More** section gives teaching suggestions on using the video effectively.

Why is it important to prepare learners before reading?

Reading is an interaction between what students already know about a topic and new material in a reading passage. They will understand and enjoy reading more if their background knowledge is drawn upon. Moreover, learners need a *reason* to read.

How should teachers use the *Warm Up* section?

Every *Reading Explorer* unit starts with a section called **Warm Up**. This helps students make connections between what they already *know*—the "K" part of the KWL approach—and the topics covered in the unit. Full-page photographs from National Geographic help students to raise interest in the unit theme, and discussion questions help students relate the reading topics to their own lives. The Teacher's Guide provides possible responses to these questions as well as additional questions that encourage students to think about the overall theme of the unit.

How should teachers use the *Before You Read* section?

Before You Read is made up of two tasks, A and B, and comes at the start of each lesson. Task A pre-teaches some key vocabulary and content that is essential to understanding the reading passage. These words (i.e., the support vocabulary) are presented in context and set in blue for emphasis. This support vocabulary appears later in the passage and is important for overall comprehension; however, it is not essential that students acquire (i.e., learn and remember) these words at this stage. More explanation about vocabulary, including the distinction between support and target vocabulary, is given on pages 12–15.

In Task A, learners complete tasks such as using the blue words to label a photograph or map, matching definitions, answering questions, or completing a short paragraph. In the process, they build visual literacy skills by reading graphically presented information, such as captions, headers, map or graph keys, just as in magazines, in newspapers, or on the Internet.

Task B provides a purpose for reading. For example, students should read the reading passage quickly to identify the main idea or make predictions about the content. Establishing what they *want* to learn is the "W" in KWL. It is important that *after* reading, teachers should take time to see what students have *learned*—"L" in KWL—from the passage.

What are the main previewing skills?

The main previewing skills are *skimming* (reading quickly for the main idea), *scanning* (reading quickly to find specific information), and *predicting* (using existing knowledge of a topic to anticipate the content of the passage). By reading quickly first, students are motivated to read more thoroughly later.

Building Learners' Reading Skills

What are the features of *Reading Explorer* texts?

Target vocabulary items are highlighted in red within the passage. They are also listed at the back of the Student Book (pages 146–147 and defined on pages 74–78 of this Teacher's Guide). These high-frequency words have been selected because they occur often in nonfiction reading. They are the useful words that students should learn and remember. Target vocabulary is developed further in the vocabulary section within each unit and recycled throughout the series.

Teachers can teach target vocabulary in various ways. Some teachers may prefer to pre-teach these words before learners read the passage; others may prefer to wait until after learners have completed a first reading of the text, before they teach or elicit the meaning of the target words.

Line numbers are provided every five lines in each reading passage. In class discussions, encourage students to use the line numbers when responding to comprehension questions. When students work in pairs, ask them to refer to the text using line numbers.

Titles and headers provide clues to the organization of a reading passage and the main ideas. Sometimes the pre-reading activities will draw special attention to them. Ask students about titles and headers after a first reading. Check whether they are able to put the headers into their own words. Typically, each paragraph has one main idea expressed in the header.

Musical Elephants

Did You Know?
Every November, thousands of people watch elephants dance and play soccer at the Surin Elephant Round-Up Festival in Thailand.

In the town of Lampang in northern Thailand, there is an unusual[1] group of musicians. They play many different kinds of music—everything from traditional Thai songs to music by Beethoven. Both children and adults love this group. What makes them so popular? Is it their music? Their looks?[2] Yes, it's both of these things, but it's also something else: they're elephants.

These musical elephants started at the Thai Elephant Conservation Center (TECC) in Lampang. The TECC protects elephants. It teaches people to understand and care for these huge, but gentle, animals. And, like many zoos around the world, the TECC encourages elephants to paint.

Richard Lair works with the TECC. He knows a lot about elephants. He says some of the animals' paintings are very good. But, in fact, elephants hear better than they see. And so he had an idea: if elephants are intelligent and they have good hearing, maybe they can play music. To test his idea, Lair and a friend started the Thai Elephant Orchestra.[3] During a performance, the elephants play a variety of instruments, including the drums and the xylophone. The animals also use their voices and trunks to make sounds.

But can elephants really make music properly? Yes, says Lair. They're very creative. Humans encourage the animals to play, but the elephants make their own songs; they don't just copy their trainers or other people. There are now CDs of the group's music, which earn money for the TECC. And the music these artists create is pretty amazing.

[1] If something is **unusual**, it does not happen very often or you do not see it or hear it very often.
[2] When you refer to someone's **looks**, you are referring to how beautiful or ugly they are.
[3] An **orchestra** is a large group of musicians who play a variety of instruments together.

1B Artistic Animals   **15**

▲ Sangduen Chailert helps elephants at a nature park near Chiang Mai, Thailand.

THAILAND

Footnote definitions for lower-frequency words (e.g., acronyms or technical terms) that are important for understanding the passage are provided at the bottom of the page.

Photographs, maps, and captions provide information that reinforces ideas from the reading passage. If students haven't been directed to use these resources in **Before You Read**, draw attention to them by asking questions that can be answered only with information found there. The Teacher's Guide provides suggestions for utilizing these resources to help promote visual literacy.

How can teachers promote reading fluency?

Reading fluency is the ability to read smoothly and effortlessly while understanding the ideas expressed in the text. To help learners achieve this goal, teachers can:

- Encourage learners to read chunks of text by phrases, rather than word by word.
- Discourage learners from "tracing" words with their fingers—or subvocalizing (reading aloud) the words while reading—as it slows down the reading process.
- In subsequent readings of the passage, have students read quickly without stopping for a timed period such as two minutes. Then check how far the learners get each time.
- Play the audio recording of the passage from the CD, and have learners read the passage at the same speed.
- Recommend that learners avoid checking each unfamiliar word in a dictionary, particularly when they read a passage for the first time.

How should teachers check reading comprehension?

Reading comprehension activities check students' understanding and their ability to use specific reading skills. The comprehension section immediately follows each reading passage. Some teachers may prefer to have students attempt to answer the questions without referring back to the text. However, note that some questions in Part A specifically refer to paragraphs or lines in the text.

How does *Reading Explorer* prepare students for standardized tests?

Reading Explorer has texts and question types similar to those used on international English exams. The labels on the questions are an effective teaching tool to familiarize students with their purposes and formats. The labels are explained in the glossary at the end of the Teacher's Guide.

Task A:

This task has five multiple-choice questions. Each one focuses on one of the following skills:

- Understanding the gist (overall theme) of the entire passage
- Choosing the main idea or the most appropriate title for the passage
- Identifying the main idea of smaller portions of text (e.g., a paragraph)
- Finding factual details (usually paraphrased from the text)
- Identifying the meaning of references in the text, e.g. pronoun references
- Understanding the meaning of vocabulary in context (different from target or support vocabulary)
- Paraphrasing ideas
- Inferring someone's intention or opinion
- Detecting the author's purpose
- Checking the accuracy of statements

Task B:

This section consists of a comprehension task that checks students' understanding of relationships between different parts of the text. Typical Part B tasks include:

- Categorizing concepts with Venn diagrams (e.g., page 12 of the Student Book)
- Sequencing information (e.g., page 22 of the Student Book)
- Sorting ideas in comparison/contrast charts (e.g., page 50 of the Student Book)
- Categorizing concept or word maps (e.g., page 36 of the Student Book)

- Understanding cause and effect with diagrams (e.g., page 138 of the Student Book)
- Matching main ideas with paragraphs (e.g., page 16 of the Student Book)
- Completing summaries with key words (e.g., page 28 of the Student Book)
- Recognizing true or false statements (e.g., page 80 of the Student Book)
- Transferring information from the reading to other text types (e.g. page 104 of the Student Book)

The use of several types of graphic organizers in Task B (Venn diagrams, flow charts, time lines, etc.) helps to further develop learners' visual literacy skills.

Additional reading comprehension questions can be found on the Student Book CD-ROM.

For further ideas on developing reading skills and fluency, see Anderson, N. J. (1999). *Exploring Second Language Reading: Issues and Strategies*. Boston: Heinle.

Developing Learners' Vocabulary

What is *Reading Explorer's* approach to language learning?

Reading Explorer aims to build the high-frequency vocabulary that learners need for academic and real-world success. The series presents words in context, and then follows with exercises that teach and recycle them. Vocabulary research has shown that both implicit and explicit instruction are important in developing vocabulary that students can retain and actively use. *Reading Explorer* provides teachers with both options.

What are the different types of vocabulary in *Reading Explorer*?

All components of *National Geographic Reading Explorer*—reading texts, video, and audio—are carefully graded to build students' vocabulary. *Reading Explorer* categorizes vocabulary into the following types:

- *Target vocabulary*: These are high-frequency words in academic and non-fiction reading. Knowing them and their related forms will help students become effective and fluent readers. Target words are highlighted in red. Target vocabulary is practiced in the **Vocabulary Practice** section of each unit of the Student Book (e.g., page 13), in the review units, and on the CD-ROM.
- *Support vocabulary*: These words appear in blue in each unit's **Before You Read** section and are accompanied by photographs and graphics that help learners understand their meaning. They pre-teach vocabulary related to the topic of the reading passage.
- *Specialized or technical vocabulary*: These are footnoted within each passage, with definitions provided beneath the text.

What are some ways to teach vocabulary in context?

When learning another language, students need specific instructions in order to build vocabulary rapidly. Guessing the meaning of unknown or new words from context works best when students have already developed a sizeable core vocabulary. For this reason, teachers may choose to pre-teach the target vocabulary before learners approach the reading. Definitions of **Target Vocabulary** are provided on pages 74–78 of this Teacher's Guide; these definitions are based on the use of the words within the reading passages.

However, even elementary and intermediate students benefit from being taught skills for understanding new vocabulary in context. Here are some suggestions for building these skills:

- Draw attention to the target vocabulary highlighted in the passage. Have students pay attention to the surrounding words. Is the new word associated or collocated with other words?
- Decide on the new word's part of speech. How does it function in the sentence? Are there clues such as articles (*an*, *the*), adjectives, adverbs, or verb endings?
- Are some components of the word familiar? Look for clues to meaning in word roots, prefixes, and suffixes.
- Is the new word defined within the text? Sometimes a synonym is given nearby in the passage.

Teaching strategies for understanding words from context will promote better reading skills. Whenever possible, encourage students to work out meaning from context without interrupting the flow of their reading. In particular, suggest that students avoid using a dictionary to look up word meanings while reading, as this will slow them down and decrease their reading fluency.

The Teacher's Guide contains suggestions for presenting and practicing vocabulary for each unit. In addition, clarifications are provided for appropriate usage and cultural considerations of certain words.

How is target vocabulary practiced and reviewed

After being presented in context in the main reading passage, target vocabulary items are subsequently recycled in several sections of the book:

1. The **Vocabulary Practice** page in each unit focuses on using the target vocabulary in various contexts. Sometimes students complete gaps in a reading with the key words. At other times, they manipulate target words or find appropriate definitions for them in context.

   Knowing a word does not just involve knowing its spelling and meaning; it is also important that learners become aware of word structure, collocations, and usage. While much of the focus of the **Vocabulary Practice** page is on word meaning, the **Vocabulary Builder** boxes supplement this by highlighting relevant word forms and associations. There are three types in Student Book 1:

   Word Link: Students develop decoding strategies based on word parts such as roots, prefixes, and suffixes.

   Word Partnerships: Common collocations and set phrases involving target vocabulary items are presented, so that learners can increase their vocabulary awareness through acquisition of lexical chunks.

   Usage: Information is provided on common usage, such as the varied meanings of a word, and the distinction between formal and slang connotations.

2. The **Explore More** section in each unit is based on a short video on a topic related to the unit theme. The video is included on both the classroom DVD and Student CD-ROM. Many of the target vocabulary items are featured on the narration of the video which has been carefully graded for language level. A summary cloze activity (Task B) recycles target vocabulary from both lessons of the unit. **Think About It** questions then give students an opportunity to use newly acquired vocabulary as they discuss the unit topic and relate it to their own lives.

   For more on using video in class, see pages 16–17 of this Teacher's Guide.

3. The **Review Unit** provides additional practice with target vocabulary.

   Each review unit starts with a crossword puzzle featuring words from the three previous units. The puzzle checks students' understanding of meanings and definitions as well as accuracy of spelling. Students can prepare for this by referring to the **Target Vocabulary** index on pages 145–147 of the Student Book. This list is cross-referenced with units and lessons. In addition, a target vocabulary list with definitions is provided on pages 74–78 of this Teacher's Guide.

The review unit continues with the completion of **Field Notes**—similar to brief notes that a researcher might make when visiting a World Heritage Site. The notes, which recycle many of the target vocabulary items from previous units, provide a model for taking notes on key information. The task relates to the following double-page **World Heritage Spotlight** section, which recycles several target vocabulary items in new contexts.

The last page of the review unit focuses on **Vocabulary Building** and consists of two sections. In Student Book 1, Task A reviews word forms described in previous units. For example, the **Word Link** section might cover suffixes such as –*tion* and –*sion* that change verbs into nouns. Students focus on individual words, then use them to complete a reading passage.

In addition, a **Word Partnership** section (Task B) introduces new word combinations, usually in the context of a reading passage relating to the topic of one of the preceding units. For example, learners identify examples of a certain word combination in a reading, then apply the combinations in a subsequent task.

4. Additional vocabulary practice exercises can be found on the **Student CD-ROM**. These interactive and self-scoring activities review the target vocabulary from the Student Book and include question types such as multiple-choice, drag and drop, and sentence completion.

What role do dictionaries play in learning?

Although target vocabulary is presented and practiced in context in *Reading Explorer*, dictionaries still play an important role in learning vocabulary. Whichever dictionary you and your students decide to use, it is important to become familiar with its features and use it regularly. Some teachers find it helpful to bring a range of dictionaries to class and develop activities that require students to contrast and compare them.

The **Vocabulary Builder** boxes found on the vocabulary practice page of the Student Book are closely based on similar features found in the Collins COBUILD range of American English dictionaries. These dictionaries are based on an extensive corpus of real-world examples and include full-sentence definitions as well as information on word origins, collocations, and usage. For more information on Collins COBUILD dictionaries, visit elt.heinle.com.

What tips can teachers offer students in learning vocabulary?

As a teacher, you can help learners become successful language learners by:

- Creating opportunities for vocabulary practice and making it fun
- Making your classroom "vocabulary rich" by placing notes and labels on walls and boards
- Creating flashcards and games (such as bingo and "hangman") as a way of reviewing recently learned vocabulary
- Including vocabulary in your assessment
- Teaching vocabulary acquisition strategies (such as learning key affixes and word roots)
- Using word webs, drawings, and other memory aids to help students remember words
- Requiring students to keep vocabulary notebooks and checking them often
- Promoting extensive reading by encouraging learners to read graded readers, such as the *Footprint Reading Library* titles listed in the list of **Recommended Graded Readers** on page 80 of this Teacher's Guide.

For further ideas on teaching vocabulary, see Nation, I. S. P. (2008). *Teaching Vocabulary: Strategies and Techniques*. Boston: Heinle.

Using Video in Class

What are the features of the *Explore More* section?

Explore More features a video with a theme related to the whole unit. It has three tasks:

- *Preview:* This section prepares students for what they will be watching.
- *Summarize:* This section requires students to complete a cloze passage that summarizes what they have watched. It recycles target vocabulary and tests students' understanding of the video.
- *Think About It*: The questions in this section allow students to think critically about what they have learned in the unit, including ideas from the video, and to relate the unit to their own lives.

All video clips are on the Student CD-ROM as well as the classroom DVD. (Note that the classroom DVD is meant for use on a regular DVD player; the video clips on the CD-ROM are for use on a computer.) The Student CD-ROM also contains additional comprehension questions about the video.

Why teach video-viewing skills?

In daily life, nonfiction videos can be found on television, on the Internet, and in theaters as documentaries. Just as *Reading Explorer* provides a wide variety of authentic text and graphic material to build students' nonfiction reading skills, the series also builds viewing skills with videos from National Geographic. *Reading Explorer* promotes visual literacy so learners can competently use a wide range of modern media.

Videos differ from word texts in important ways. First, students are processing information by viewing and listening simultaneously. Visual images include information about the video's setting as well as nonverbal communication such as facial expressions and body movements. The soundtrack contains narration, conversations, music, and sound effects. Some contextual words may appear on screen in signs or as identification of people or settings. In addition, full English subtitles ("closed captions") are available as a teaching and learning option.

What are the stages of viewing?

Previewing prepares students for the video, engages their background knowledge about the topic, and creates interest in what they will watch. Effective ways of previewing include:

- Brainstorming and discussing about what the class already knows about the topic
- Using photographs and the video's title to predict the content
- Pre-teaching key vocabulary essential to understanding the video content
- Skimming the summary reading

Viewing may occur multiple times and at different speeds while:

- Watching for gist comprehension of the main ideas from the film
- Watching and listening closely for detail
- Watching and listening for opinion and inference

Post-viewing activities include:

- Describing the main points and the sequence of events in the video
- Completing the cloze summary with provided target vocabulary
- Answering **Think About It** questions that relate the video to the students' own lives or experiences

How should teachers use the videos to teach?

The narration on each video has been carefully graded to feature vocabulary and structures that are appropriate for students' proficiency level. The location of the video section at the end of each unit ensures that students already bring background knowledge and target vocabulary to the viewing process.

Here are techniques for using video in class:

- Have students preview the video by reading the transcript or the summary paragraph.
- Pause, rewind, or fast-forward the video to focus on key segments or events.
- Pause the video midway to allow students to predict what will happen next. Resume the video so students can check their predictions.
- Have students watch the video with the sound muted, to focus only on what they see. If this approach is used, follow-up discussion helps students share their ideas about the content of the video. Then play with sound for students to check their ideas.
- Have students watch without subtitles after which they make predictions about what they will hear; then play with subtitles for students to check their predictions.
- Have students follow the script as they listen to the video to help in improving intonation, pitch, and stress. Stop and replay key phrases for students to repeat.
- Have students watch the video independently and complete the comprehension questions on the Student CD-ROM.

Note that the cloze summary (Task B of **Explore More**) can be used without the video if desired. All video scripts are printed on pages 148–159 of the Student Book. Teachers have flexibility in how or whether they want students to use the scripts. See individual units in this Teacher's Guide for specific teaching suggestions for each video.

To extend viewing skills to speaking and writing skills, have students make a presentation or create a written report, about a short video of their choice, using language they have learned from the Student Book and video narration.

Exploring Further: Reading and Viewing

How else can students improve their reading skills and increase their awareness of the world?

1. The review units in *Reading Explorer* further develop learners' reading skills and visual literacy through the use of graphic images such as charts, diagrams, maps, and symbols. In addition, one of the aims of *Reading Explorer* includes motivating students to learn about the world and its cultures. Features of the course that promote these goals are:

- Spotlights on UNESCO (United Nations Educational, Scientific, and Cultural Organization) World Heritage Sites in each review unit
- Extensive reading on related topics through the *Footprint Reading Library*
- *Reading Explorer* website with student search activities and downloadable materials for teachers

The review units highlight well-known places of outstanding cultural or natural importance that have been designated UNESCO World Heritage Sites. Features of the review units include:

- Full-color, two-page spreads with maps and 3-D drawings
- Descriptions of unique features
- Information on location and status
- Glossary of special terms (highlighted in blue in the text)
- Field Notes sections that summarize facts about the sites

2. The *Footprint Reading Library* is a series of graded readers produced through collaboration between Heinle Cengage Learning and National Geographic. *Footprint* readers, audio, and visual materials are controlled for vocabulary and grammatical structures appropriate for learners' proficiency levels. See page 80 of this Teacher's Guide for suggested extensive readers from the *Footprint Reading Library* for each unit.

3. Both teachers and learners are encouraged to use the *Reading Explorer* website (elt.heinle.com) for further independent reading and exploration opportunities, and also National Geographic's main website: Nationalgeographic.com. The National Geographic website offers many short videos on topics closely related to *Reading Explorer* topics. These videos provide opportunities for independent learning and extension activities.

Assessing Learners' Progress

How can learners' progress be assessed with *Reading Explorer*?

Ongoing assessment with *Reading Explorer* allows teachers to obtain feedback on students' progress in vocabulary, reading skills, and visual literacy. Ways that teachers can assess learners include:

- Reading comprehension questions that reflect current question formats on standardized English exams
- Vocabulary practice and review sections that check learners' understanding of recently acquired vocabulary
- Self-grading vocabulary activities and reading and viewing comprehension questions on the Student CD-ROM
- Web search activities that enable teachers to monitor students' progress in learning independently
- Assessment CD-ROM with Exam*View*® so teachers can quickly create customized tests

The Exam*View*® software provided with *Reading Explorer* contains banks of questions on readings and vocabulary for each unit. The questions mirror many of the types and formats of questions used in the Student Book. With Exam*View*®, teachers can create and customize exams quickly and easily.

The Exam*View*® component provides the following question banks for each unit of *Reading Explorer*:

- An additional reading passage related to the unit topic with 10 comprehension questions
- A bank of 10 questions relating to the target vocabulary of Lesson A
- A bank of 10 questions relating to the target vocabulary of Lesson B

The questions cover a variety of task types, including multiple-choice, true/false, and completion. The reading comprehension questions focus on the same range of reading skills that are highlighted in the Student Book, for example, understanding main ideas, details, and inferences, identifying references, and understanding vocabulary from context.

Unit Introduction

This unit focuses on animal intelligence. Students will read about several intelligent animals, including bottlenose dolphins, orangutans, chimps, Asian elephants, and macaque monkeys.

Key Words for Internet Research: *animal intelligence, chimp computer, dolphin communication, elephant musician, macaque learning, orangutan sign language*

For More Information: http://ngm.nationalgeographic.com/2008/03/animal-minds/virginia-morell-text/1

Warm Up

Answer Key

Possible responses are: **1.** Humans use a full range of language skills, deal with abstract thoughts and things that are not physically present, refer to the past and the future, and invent and design complex machines and buildings; **2.** Animals rely more heavily on innate or inborn behaviors and are able to function on their own shortly after birth. Moreover, their senses of sight, smell, and sound are often greater than human senses; **3.** Answers will vary, but ask students to provide *reasons* for their choice.

Teaching Notes

Write the word *monkey* on the board and pronounce the name *proboscis* [pro **bahs** is]. Tell students to look at the photo and read the caption. Ask them:
- **What is the animal in the photo doing?** leaping through the air, carrying its baby
- **What kind of animal is it?** a proboscis monkey
- **Where is Sabah?** in the northeast of the island of Borneo near Brunei; it's a Malaysian state
- **What kind of place is it?** a rain forest and jungle
- **Can you find another animal in the unit that lives in Borneo?** the orangutan on page 13

Ask students what is unusual about these monkeys (their large noses and their ability to leap long distances).

Lesson 1A Animal Intelligence

Lesson Overview

Target Vocabulary:

advantage, alike, assist, conversation, intelligent, method, smart, specific, strategy, system

Reading Passage Summary:

Like humans, dolphins can plan, communicate ideas, and have fun.

Answer Key

Before You Read

A.* **1.** T; **2.** T; **3.** T; **4.** F. Most bottlenose dolphins live in groups, called pods.
B. b. things dolphins do

Reading Comprehension

A. 1. a; **2.** b (lines 10–14); **3.** b (lines 26–30); **4.** c; **5.** a
B. Humans: c; Dolphins: g; Both: a, b, d, e, f, and h

Vocabulary Practice

A. 1. intelligent; **2.** strategy; **3.** system; **4.** conversation
B. 1. method; **2.** assist; **3.** alike; **4.** advantage;
   5. specific; **6.** smart

---

*These answers are also available in the Student Book on page 18.

Teaching Notes

Before You Read

A. True or False: Say the word *dolphin* [**doll** fin] with students and ask what they know about these animals. Have students complete Activity A. Check answers as a class.

Mammals (Question 1) are warm-blooded animals that have live babies instead of laying eggs as fish do. Female mammals feed their babies milk. A *whistle* (Question 2) can be a noise-making tube as shown on page 10, or it can be the kind of sound made by animals as mentioned in Question 3. Question 4 contrasts *live by themselves* with the photo caption of dolphins as *social animals* that prefer to be with other animals instead of being alone.

B. Skim for the Main Idea: Remind students that skimming means reading a passage *quickly* to get the main idea. Allow students 30 seconds to read as quickly as they can, then have them close their books. On the board, poll students' answers for Activity B. Ask students to open their books and say which clues helped them identify the main idea. The answer, b. things dolphins do, indicates that verbs such as *communicate*, *play*, and *help* are important clues.

If students have difficulty identifying the main idea, ask them what sorts of information would be needed to support the other two options. For example, for "types of dolphins" you would expect to see names and descriptions of different kinds of dolphins. For the option "what dolphins eat," note that while the last paragraph does mention that dolphins eat fish, in this case, the main idea is supposed to apply to the entire reading passage.

Reading Comprehension

A. Multiple Choice: Have students read the entire passage silently and answer the questions for Activity A. Check answers as a class, asking students to give evidence for their answers from the reading passage.

Note that *language* (Question 2) may mean many ways of communicating other than human speech. For example, the photo caption on page 11 says that dolphins use *body language* to communicate.

Ask students to give some examples of body language (facial expressions, posture, signals such as waving, etc.).

B. Classification: If students are unfamiliar with Venn diagrams, point out that the overlapping area is for traits or characteristics that both groups share in common. Have students complete Activity B. Check answers as a class.

Challenge: Write the following questions on the board for early finishers. Additional comprehension questions are available on the CD-ROM.
1. Do you think dolphins really are intelligent? Why or why not?
2. How do you think human intelligence is different from animal intelligence?

Vocabulary Practice

A. Completion: Review vocabulary by talking about the reading on dolphins from page 11. Give students the example: *Dolphins are <u>intelligent</u> because they play together*. In pairs, ask students to create three sentences about dolphins using vocabulary from page 13. Share answers as a class. Have students do Activity A.

B. Matching: Point out antonym pairs: *alike/different*, *intelligent/unintelligent*, *smart/stupid*, *specific/vague*, *advantage/disadvantage*. Have students do Activity B. Check answers as a class.

Challenge: Ask early finishers to talk quietly about other animals using the vocabulary words on page 13.

Word Link

Write the following words on the board: *appearance*, *difference*, *entrance*, *performance*. Have students study the word parts (e.g., appear + ance, enter + ance). Ask them to use the words to complete sentences you make up (e.g., "The _____ to the school is in the front of the building."). Invite students to make their own sentences.

Lesson 1B Artistic Animals

Lesson Overview

Target Vocabulary:

artist, creative, earn, encourage, gentle, huge, performance, popular, properly, trainer

Reading Passage Summary:

Elephants at a conservation center in Thailand paint pictures and play in an elephant orchestra.

Answer Key

Before You Read

A. Students label the photograph: **1.** trunk; **2.** xylophone; **3.** elephant; **4.** instruments; **5.** drum
B. paint, play music, play soccer

Reading Comprehension

A. 1. d; **2.** b; **3.** c; **4.** b; **5.** a
B. Paragraph 1. b; Paragraph 2. e; Paragraph 3. a; Paragraph 4. d

Vocabulary Practice

A. 1. trainers; **2.** encourage; **3.** creative; **4.** artists; **5.** earn
B. 1. a; **2.** a; **3.** a; **4.** b; **5.** a

Teaching Notes

Before You Read

A. Labeling: *Instruments* is a group term for a variety of specific instruments such as drum or xylophone. Ask if anyone knows how the instruments in the picture are played. Can they demonstrate how to play the instruments? Have students do Activity A. Check answers as a class.

B. Predict: Have students do Activity B. Ask them to cite evidence from the photo to support their answers. Check answers as a class.

Reading Comprehension

A. Multiple Choice: Have students read the passage and complete Activity A. Check answers as a class.

In Question 4, *variety* means many (certainly more than two) different kinds of something. Some English language learners confuse *too* with *very* as an intensifier and therefore might be tempted to choose option "d," so point out that *too many* means an excessive number. For Question 5, ask students to say what the last sentence means in their own words. Option "c" is meant to appeal to students who are reading literally and might equate *pretty* with *beautiful*.

B. Matching: Point out that most paragraphs are built around one main idea that is often expressed in a topic sentence at the start of a paragraph. If students are confused between main ideas "a" and "b,"

have them decide which paragraph is more general (the first one) and which paragraph deals primarily with the work of one man (the third). Have students do Activity B. Check answers as a class.

Challenge: For students interested in doing more with the topic, ask the following questions:

Would you go to a Thai Elephant Orchestra concert or buy one of its CDs? Why or why not?

Vocabulary Practice

A. Completion: In pairs, have students write short summaries of the reading on page 15. Ask them to try to use all of the vocabulary words at the top of page 17. Ask pairs to volunteer to read their examples to the class. Have students do Activity A. Check answers as a class.

Mention the word *artist* is often used for a person who creates a work of art such as a drawing or painting. However, it can also mean a performer such as a musician, an actor, or a dancer. In the reading on page 17, the creative elephants are artists in two ways—as painters and as musicians.

B. Words in Context: Point out antonym pairs: *encourage/discourage*, *popular/unpopular*, *creative/dull*, *gentle/rough*, *huge/tiny*, *properly/improperly*. Have students do Activity B. Check answers as a class.

Mention *huge* often refers to enormous size, as for elephants. However, it can also mean something extreme in amount or degree. As an adverb, it is often used to mean *extremely*. For example: *The new band is <u>hugely</u> popular, and tickets are sold out for all their performances*. Informally, people sometimes reply *It's <u>huge</u>!* when they are asked how important something is. That means it is very important.

Challenge: For early finishers, write the following questions on the board. Additional vocabulary questions are available on the CD-ROM.
1. How have elephants learned to paint? Are all elephants creative? In what ways?
2. An elephant did the painting shown on the page 17 ("Green Symphony"). Is it really art?

Word Link

The suffix *-ist* means someone who does something, often as a job or occupation. Ask students if they know any other jobs that end in *-ist*. Write jobs like *dentist, receptionist, hairstylist, pharmacist,* and *florist* on the board and have students use them to complete sentences like the following:
A _____ sells flowers.
A _____ cleans your teeth.
A _____ answers the phone calls in a company.
A _____ cuts your hair.
You buy medicine from a _____.

 # Explore More

Video Summary: In Surat Thani, Thailand, monkeys learn how to pick coconuts from tall trees.

Answer Key

A. 1. monkey; **2.** trainer; **3.** coconut; **4.** rope
B. 1. intelligent; **2.** trainer; **3.** encourages; **4.** advantage;
    5. method; **6.** popular; **7.** huge; **8.** earn;
    9. assistance

C. 1. Somporn Saewkwo trains monkeys this way:
- First, he holds the monkey's hands.
- Next, he shows the animal how to spin a coconut to take it from a tree.
- Later, he takes the monkey to a high tree, and he encourages the animal to climb up to pick the fruit. The monkey wears a rope, so Saewkwo can direct the animal from the ground.

   2. Answers will vary but should include an example that indicates intelligence.

Teaching Notes

A. Preview: For suggestions on building students' viewing skills, see pages 15–16.

Have students complete Activity A before they discuss the title of the video. In this context, a *trainer* Is like a teacher. Check that students understand a *college* usually means an institution where students study after they finish high school. What do they think the video is going to be about? Check answers as a class.

B. Summarize: Follow these steps:
   1. Students watch the video through once, bearing in mind the answers they gave in the **Preview**.

   2. Before playing the video a second time, ask students to read the summary and fill the gaps in Activity B with vocabulary items from the box. They close their books while watching the video.
   3. After they've watched the video a second time, students complete or change their answers on the summary. Have them check answers with a partner.
   4. If necessary, play the video through a third time and then check answers as a class.

C. Think About It: Have students answer the questions in Activity C in pairs. Discuss ideas as a class.

Unit Introduction

The focus of this unit is adventure travel. Students will read about traveling the length of the Americas by bicycle, surfing volcanoes, diving on land in the South Pacific, and running with bulls in Spain.

Key Words for Internet Research: *adventure travel, Brooks Allen, bungee jumping, Gregg Bleakney, hiking safety, land diving, running of the bulls, San Fermín, travel abroad, Vanuatu, volcano surfing*

For More Information: http://adventure.nationalgeographic.com/

Warm Up

Answer Key

Answers will vary.

Teaching Notes

Write the words *cave* and *Oman* on the board and pronounce the country's name [oh **mahn**]. Direct students' attention to the photo and have them read the caption. Ask them:
- **Where is Oman?** The country is at the end of the Arabian peninsula on the Indian Ocean.
- **What is the man in the photo doing?** lowering himself into a cave
- **Why do people explore caves?** to see underground water and unusual formations such as *stalactites* and *stalagmites*, to search for ancient artifacts, to find out where the cave goes
- **How is the man in the photo dressed?** He is wearing equipment to explore the cave—he has a hard hat with a light on it, a pack that probably contains ropes and gear, and it also looks like he is wearing a special suit.

The name of the cave in the photo, Majlis al Jinn, means "the living room of the spirits" in Arabic. Ask students what they think the scientist might find inside the cave.

Lesson 2A | Adventure Destinations

Lesson Overview

Target Vocabulary:

abroad, advice, ancient, baggage, especially, eventually, formed, polite, relaxed, trip

Reading Passage Summary:

Two friends bike from Alaska to Argentina.

Answer Key

Before You Read

A. hike, camp, cruise, swim
B. 1. They started in Prudhoe Bay, Alaska, and ended in Ushuaia, Argentina. They rode bikes; **2.** They traveled 30,500 km or 19,000 miles.

Reading Comprehension

A. 1. a; **2.** d (lines 19–21); **3.** b (lines 11–12); **4.** a; **5.** c
B. 4 (from map), 6 (lines 18–19), 1 (lines 4–5), 2 (lines 6–7), 5 (lines 19–21), 3 (lines 8–9)

Vocabulary Practice

A. 1. ancient; **2.** formed; **3.** abroad
B. 1. advice; **2.** especially; **3.** baggage; **4.** trip; **5.** relax; **6.** eventually

Teaching Notes

Before You Read

A. Completion: Encourage students to comment on the photographs and guess which continent they are on (Columbia is in South America, Mongolia in Asia, Senegal in Africa, and Albania in Europe). Ask what students see in the photographs. You may need to supply vocabulary such as mountain path or trail, sand dune, rain forest, chimpanzee, and so on. Have students complete Activity A. Check answers as a class. As students read their completed sentences, point out collocations with the words around the gaps such as *hike through mountains*, *camp in a tent*, *take a riverboat cruise*, and *swim in blue waters*.

B. Scan: Remind students that scanning means reading quickly to find specific information. See page 9 for suggestions on pre-reading strategies. Ask what kinds of words give clues about starting and ending points, means of travel, and distance. Have students complete Activity B. Some distance words they may mention are *from*, *to*, *eventually reached*, and *km* or *miles*. Check answers as a class.

Students may respond with very general information. Encourage them to use the map for more detailed information such as Prudhoe Bay or Ushuaia [oo **swai** uh]. In lines 19–21 of the reading, students learn that Brooks had to stop in Guatemala. Ask if students know where Guatemala is (it's a country in Central America, just south of Mexico on the map). AL and CA are abbreviations for Alaska and California—two states in the United States.

Reading Comprehension

A. Multiple Choice: Ask students to read the entire passage silently and answer the questions for Activity A. Check answers as a class, asking students to give evidence for their answers from the reading passage.

Note that Question 2 asks students to identify which sentence is false or not true, meaning that three sentences are true. Refer students to paragraph 1 where the full names of the two men appear. Then, note that for the rest of the reading, they are referred to only by first name. Accurate readers will see in lines 19–21 that it was Brooks who got sick and had to return home.

Question 5 on inference can be best answered by re-reading Gregg's advice about traveling in lines 25–32. Options "b" and "d" are contradicted by his advice and option "a" is the opposite of what Gregg actually did on his long trip (lines 9–12).

B. Sequencing: Remind students that some events will take place before the actual bicycle trip. Have students complete Activity B. Ask students to work in pairs to check their sequences by retelling the story in the reading.

Challenge: For students who have completed Activities A and B, write the following question on the board. Additional comprehension questions are available on the CD-ROM.

The reading says Gregg stopped in 12 countries. Compare the map on page 21 to an atlas and list the countries you think he traveled through.

(**Answer:** He traveled through the United States, Canada, Mexico, Guatemala, Nicaragua, Costa Rica, Panama, Ecuador, Peru, Bolivia, Chile, and Argentina.)

Vocabulary Practice

A. Definitions: Point out antonym pairs: *abroad/locally*, *ancient/modern*, *formed/destroyed*. Have students do Activity A. Check answers as a class.

B. Completion: Have students do Activity B. Check answers as a class. You may want to mention that *baggage* is a noncount noun, so it has the same form in both singular and plural. In its physical meaning, it refers to travelers' luggage or suitcases. In travel contexts, the word collocates as *baggage car*, a train car where baggage is stored and *baggage claim*, the place in an airport where you collect your checked luggage. In another sense, *baggage* refers to the set of mental attitudes or prejudices that people carry around with them. *Al carries around so much baggage from his childhood.*

Challenge: For students who have completed Activities A and B, write the following questions on the board. Additional vocabulary questions are available on the CD-ROM.

1. How does the map on page 23 fit into the map on page 21?

2. Would you like to visit Patagonia? Why or why not?

Usage

The noun *advice* is both singular and plural. It never takes an "s" at the end. People *ask for advice*, *give advice*, or *take advice*. Advice is a personal opinion about what someone should do/should not do in a situation. The suggestion provides guidance, but whether or not to follow advice is a voluntary matter. Some newspapers have an advice column about personal matters like relationships.

Extreme Activities

Lesson Overview

Target Vocabulary:

century, escape, extreme, familiar, goal, hit, native, religious, strength, tie

Reading Passage Summary:

The South Pacific nation of Vanuatu [**van** wha too] offers visitors two of the most exciting and dangerous activities in the world: volcano surfing and land diving.

Answer Key

Before You Read

A. 1. Tonga, Vanuatu, New Zealand; **2.** a, c, b, d
B. b. dangerous

Reading Comprehension

A. 1. b; **2.** c (lines 10–11); **3.** d (lines 19–20); **4.** a; **5.** b
B. Volcano surfing: b, c, and f; Land diving: a, d, and e; Both: g

Vocabulary Practice

A. 1. religious; **2.** familiar; **3.** tie; **4.** goal; **5.** escape; **6.** hit; **7.** century; **8.** natives; **9.** strength
B. 1. century; **2.** escape; **3.** goal; **4.** native; **5.** hit; **6.** familiar; **7.** tie

Teaching Notes

Before You Read

A. Matching: Write the words *extreme activities* on the board and ask the students what these mean. The word *extreme* means "far beyond the norm." Some students will be familiar with *extreme sports* such as skydiving, bungee jumping, and bicycle motocross racing from the X Games. These sports have a high degree of danger because of unpredictable factors. Have students complete Activity A. Check answers as a class.

Snorkeling uses a face mask, breathing tube, and foot fins to enable a person to swim slightly below the surface of the water to watch fish and see coral. It differs from scuba diving that requires more complicated equipment such as an air tank and vest. However, scuba divers can go much deeper underwater because they have an air supply.

Bungee jumping starts by attaching a stretchable cord to the ankles while standing on a high platform or bridge. When the person jumps, the elastic cord takes up some of the energy and the person "bounces" while still safely attached to the high structure.

B. Main Idea: Have students answer the question in Activity B. Check answers as a class. Ask students to give evidence to support their answers.

Reading Comprehension

A. Multiple Choice: Have students read the passage and complete Activity A. Check answers as a class.

For Question 2, students must decide which of the four sentences about Mount Yasur is correct. In the reading passage, lines 8–11 state that it is an active volcano on Tanna Island, so options "a" and "d" are eliminated. The same part of the text says that people have climbed the mountain for centuries, so option "c" is a true statement—as long as readers understand that a century covers 100 years.

The reference Question 4 is a little different from many reference questions because it does not have an antecedent in the passage. Instead, the word *people* is implied in the phrase ". . . for those (people) interested in adventure and sport . . ." in lines 2 and 3.

B. Classification: Have students do Activity B. A Venn diagram is used to compare and contrast volcano surfing and land diving. In the reading, there is no indication that only men do volcano surfing. Check answers as a class.

Challenge: For students interested in doing more with the topic, ask the following questions:
1. How are volcano surfing and land diving similar to and different from the water versions?

2. Does volcano surfing sound interesting to you? Would you try it? Explain your answer.

Additional reading comprehension questions are available on the CD-ROM.

Vocabulary Practice

A. Completion: Have students complete the sentences in Activity A. Check answers as a class. Mention that English has several time-period words: *decade* for 10 years, *century* for 100 years, and *millennium* for 1,000 years. The number of the century refers to the previous 100 years. For example, the twentieth century covers the time from 1900 to 1999. We are now in the twenty-first century.

B. Definitions: Have students complete the definitions in Activity B. Check answers as a class.

Challenge: For students who have completed Activities A and B, write the following questions on the board. Additional vocabulary questions are available on the CD-ROM.

Pretend you just watched the running of the bulls in Pamplona. Write an e-mail describing the event.
1. What happened? What was the goal of the event?
2. How close were the bulls to the runners?

Word Partnership

A *native* is someone who was born in a particular area. *Maria is a native of Argentina.* Plants and animals can also be *native species*, found naturally in a location. *Rhubarb is a native plant of Siberia.* Your native language is the first language you learned as a child. *Magumi's native language is Japanese, but she speaks English and German very well.*

Explore More

Video Summary: On Pentecost Island, people still perform the original form of bungee jumping—a ritual known as the Naghol.

Answer Key

A. 1. a; **2.** b
B. 1. extreme; **2.** century; **3.** religious; **4.** advice; **5.** relax; **6.** especially; **7.** hit; **8.** natives; **9.** tie; **10.** goal

C. 1. It was a religious and fertility ritual that also tested men's bravery.
   2. Answers will vary according to personal opinion, but responses should say why an activity is the most dangerous.

Teaching Notes

A. Preview: For suggestions on building students' viewing skills, see pages 15–16. In this case, students already have background knowledge about land diving from the **Reading Passage**. To prepare them for the video, ask how land diving compares with bungee jumping (pictured in **Before You Read**).

Ask students to look at the visuals on page 28 for the context of the video. Compare the map of the Vanuatu island group with the map on page 24. What kind of a place do they think they'll see? Will it be a modern place or a traditional one? (Vanuatu is a traditional society with a chief as the political leader.) Ask students to answer the two questions in Activity A. Check answers as a class.

B. Summarize: Follow these steps:
   1. Students watch the video through once, bearing in mind the answers they gave in the **Preview**.

   2. Before playing the video a second time, ask students to read the summary and fill the gaps in Activity B with vocabulary items from the box. They close their books while watching the video.
   3. After they've watched the video a second time, students complete or change their answers on the summary. Have them check answers with a partner.
   4. If necessary, play the video through a third time and then check answers as a class.

C. Think About It: Have students answer the questions in Activity C in pairs. Discuss ideas as a class.

Unit Introduction

This unit explores how hip-hop music from New York has merged with local traditions in Dakar, Senegal, the Czech Republic, and Palestine. The unit then explores Carnival music, Brazilian samba reggae, and Caribbean steel drum music.

Key Words for Internet Research: *Assane N'Diaye, Brazilian samba reggae, Caribbean steel drums, Carlinhos Brown, Carnival music, gypsies, hip-hop, rap, Roma, Shameema Williams*

For More Information: http://worldmusic.nationalgeographic.com/worldmusic/view/page.basic/home

Warm Up

Answer Key

Possible responses are: **1.** Kinds of music include rock, jazz, hip-hop, rap, pop, and classical. Favorites may include individual performers or groups. **2.** A concert is a public performance of an artist or group for an audience. Some rock concerts have thousands of people in the audience. **3.** An example is the Festival of World Music in Fez, Morocco. Some festivals, such as Thailand's *Loy Krathong* autumn moon celebration, are not musical.

Teaching Notes

Write the place name *Bahia* on the board and pronounce the name [bah **ee** ah]. Direct students' attention to the photo and have them read the caption. Ask them:

- **What are the people in the photo doing?** dancing in a street festival
- **What is a street festival?** a big outdoor party in the streets, a parade everyone can join
- **What are the dancers wearing?** costumes, hair ornaments, and a lot of makeup
- **Where is Bahia?** Bahia is a state in eastern Brazil. Portuguese explorers landed there in 1500 and later brought slaves from West Africa to work on the sugar plantations. Today, Bahia has a richly mixed culture from many different traditions.
- **Can you find Bahia in other places in this unit?** pages 35 and 37

Ask about what other places students know in Brazil (São Paulo, Rio de Janiero).

Lesson 3A | A World of Music

Lesson Overview

Target Vocabulary:

attitudes, audience, background, belong (to), clubs, despite, face, female, issues, peace

Reading Passage Summary:

People describe hip-hop music in their countries.

Answer Key

Before You Read

A. 1. rhythm; **2.** teenagers; **3.** hardships; **4.** slaves
B. c. Hip-hop in two countries

Reading Comprehension

A. 1. c; **2.** d (line 9); **3.** b (lines 13–15); **4.** d (lines 20–28); **5.** d
B. 1. Assane N'Diaye: b and c; **2.** Shameema: a and d; **3.** Both: e

Vocabulary Practice

A. 1. female; **2.** belongs; **3.** club; **4.** background; **5.** Despite
B. 1. issues; **2.** face; **3.** peace; **4.** attitudes; **5.** audiences

Teaching Notes

Before You Read

A. Matching: Unit 3A opens with a timeline with markings by centuries until 1900, then by decades. Eight different kinds or *genres* of music are shown in red. Ask students what they know about these types of music. For example, people with African roots have played a leading role in most of these genres. Write the name of each genre on the board and encourage students to give names of artists or groups that play that kind of music. Examples are B.B. King for *blues* or Bob Marley for *reggae*. Have students do Activity A. Check answers as a class.

B. Skim for the Main Idea: Remind students that skimming means reading a passage *quickly* to get the main idea. See page 9 for suggestions on pre-reading strategies. Have students do Activity B. Check answers as a class. Select students to tell the class about clues that helped them to understand the main idea of the reading passage.

Reading Comprehension

Hip-hop music features *rap* or speaking in rhythm over a musical background created by a DJ (disc jockey) as pictured on page 30. Write the names *Assane N'Diaye* [ah **san** ng **die** yeah], *Shameema* [shah **me** mah] *Williams*, and *Czech* [check] on the board and pronounce them.

- Ask students to guess where Senegal (West Africa) and the Czech Republic (Eastern Europe) are, then check responses with the globe maps. The situation of hip-hop music in these places is called *scenes*. Understanding this is important for Question 1 on the purpose of the reading.
- Note that *tolerance* and *discrimination* are opposites. *Tolerance* is a positive acceptance of others, while *discrimination* is negative actions toward other people. The *Roma* or *gypsies* often face *prejudice* or *discrimination* in Europe. Prejudice is the mental attitude and discrimination is actions based on the attitude.

A. Multiple Choice: Have students read the entire passage silently and complete Activity A. Question 3 entails a process of elimination as students read each option and compare it with Assane N'Diaye's statements and attitudes in lines 13–15. Check answers as a class.

For Question 4, students identify which options are true in order to find the false one. Option "a" is in lines 27–28, option "b" in lines 20–21, and option "c" in lines 23–24. Point out that comprehension questions will often paraphrase words with synonyms, such as *dislike* for *discrimination*.

B. Classification: Have students do Activity B. Check answers as a class. Ask students to support their classification in Activity B by giving line numbers to support their answers. For item "d" make sure they understand that Senegal is in West Africa, not South Africa.

Challenge: For students who have completed Activities A and B, write the following question on the board. Additional comprehension questions are available on the CD-ROM.

Do you think rap music can change people's lives? Explain why or why not.

Vocabulary Practice

A. Completion: Have students complete the sentences in Activity A. Check answers as a class. *Despite* is a preposition commonly used at the beginning of a sentence to introduce a fact that makes something surprising. *Despite being only 1.5 meters tall, Mario was a great basketball player.*

B. Completion: Have students complete the sentences in Activity B. Check answers as a class. An *issue* is an important subject that people are talking or writing about. As a noun, it can also be the version of a newspaper or magazine that is published on a certain date. Informally, issue has come to mean problems. *The kindergarten teacher talked with Bob's mother about his behavioral issues.* As a verb, issue means to give out something. *The post office issued a new stamp yesterday.*

Challenge: For students who have completed Activities A and B, write the following questions on the board. Additional vocabulary questions are available on the CD-ROM.
1. What's DAM's background? Where are they from? (they're from Palestine in the Middle East)
2. What do they rap about? Give some examples. (social problems that women and youth face, the need for greater tolerance and understanding)

Usage

Sex is the term used for biological classification of individuals as *male* or *female* according to their physical characteristics.

Carnival Time!

Lesson Overview

Target Vocabulary:

differ, fill, heavily, influenced, invented, lively, mix, organization, population, region

Reading Passage Summary:

Bahia, a region in eastern Brazil, is the home of samba reggae, a mix of African, Caribbean, and South American musical styles.

Answer Key

Before You Read

A. Answers will vary. Possible answers are: All of the festivals have parades. The celebrations in New Orleans, Venice, and Rio all feature costumes. Elaborate costumes are also worn in Port of Spain, but that is not indicated in the text or photo. Three of the sites have a particular kind of music (jazz, soca, and samba), but nothing is mentioned about music in Venice. Venice is unique in that its festival occurs on boats.

B. b. a type of music

Reading Comprehension

A. 1. b; **2.** c (lines 16–17); **3.** a (line 20); **4.** b (lines 15–16); **5.** a (line 17)

B. 6. eastern (line 11); **7.** drums (lines 18–19); **8.** Jamaican reggae (lines 16–17); **9.** invented (lines 21–22); **10.** (local) organizations (lines 23–25)

Vocabulary Practice

A. 1. mix; **2.** lively; **3.** region; **4.** influenced; **5.** organization

B. 1. b; **2.** a; **3.** a; **4.** b; **5.** a

Teaching Notes

Before You Read

A. Discussion: Have students answer the questions in Activity A. They will compare and contrast four different festivals. Check answers as a class.

B. Skim for the Main Idea: Remind students that skimming means reading a passage *quickly* to get the main idea. See page 9 for suggestions on pre-reading strategies. Have students do Activity B. Select students to tell the class about clues that helped them to understand the main idea of the reading passage.

Reading Comprehension

A. Multiple Choice: Have students do Activity A. For Question 1 about main idea, note that individual statements can be true without being the main idea of the reading. Check answers as a class.

B. Summary: Have students complete Activity B. Encourage students to complete the blanks with their own words before turning back to the reading

passage. It is acceptable for students to use synonyms that have the same sense as the original words. Check answers as a class.

Challenge: For students interested in doing more with the topic, ask the following questions. Additional comprehension questions are available on the CD-ROM.
1. Describe samba reggae. What types of music influenced it? What does it sound like? What are the most important instruments?
2. Choose a type of music that you like. Where and how was that type of music first created?

Vocabulary Practice

A. Completion: Have students use the vocabulary words to complete the sentences in Activity A.

B. Words in Context: Have students do Activity B. Note that *population* can refer to the number of people who live in a particular place or to the subgroups who live there.

If you *invent* something, you are the first person to make it or to think of it. However, if you *discover* something, the thing already exists and you are the first one to learn about it.

Challenge: For students who have completed Activities A and B, write the following questions on the board. Additional vocabulary questions are available on the CD-ROM.
1. Where is Carlinhos Brown from? What is his music like?
2. Does your country have a special kind of music? Describe it.

Explore More

Video Summary: The country of Trinidad and Tobago invented a musical instrument called *steelband*. Learn about its history and the importance of this music to the people of Trinidad.

Answer Key

A. Oil drums called *pans* are hammered until they are tuned to certain pitches. The pans come in different sizes and are usually played by a large group of performers.

B. 1. lively; **2.** fills; **3.** backgrounds; **4.** invented; **5.** influenced; **6.** region; **7.** Despite; **8.** belongs to

C. 1. If you "play music by ear," you play music by listening to it. You do not read music.
  2. Steelband music is mostly instrumental instead of a combination of singing and instruments. A steelband group has mostly one kind of instrument, many steel drums of different sizes.

Teaching Notes

A. Preview: For suggestions on building students' viewing skills, see pages 15–16. Have students answer the question in Activity A.

Trinidad and Tobago, located off the northeast coast of South America, is a Caribbean country. It is an oil producer and uses large steel drums for shipping oil. A specialist in tuning steel drums hammers each drum until certain spots on the surface produce pitches in a musical scale that increases by halftones. The skilled "man with a hammer" can become more famous than a steelband player.

B. Summarize: Follow these steps:
  1. Students watch the video through once, bearing in mind the answers they gave in the **Preview**.

2. Before playing the video a second time, ask students to read the summary and fill the gaps in Activity B with vocabulary items from the box. They close their books while watching the video.
3. After they've watched the video a second time, students complete or change their answers on the summary. Have them check answers with a partner.
4. Students read the video transcript on page 150 to help understand the Trinidadian dialect.
5. If necessary, play the video through a third time and then check answers as a class.

C. Think About It: Have students answer the questions in Activity C in pairs. Discuss ideas as a class.

Answer Key

A. Across: **1.** advantage; **4.** assist; **7.** encourage; **8.** population; **9.** extreme; **11.** century; **13.** peace; **14.** huge; **15.** fill; **16.** invent; **17.** popular; **18.** mix
Down: **1.** abroad; **2.** ancient; **3.** eventually; **5.** smart; **6.** audience; **10.** escape; **12.** region; **15.** form
B. Andes, 1450, Inca, 300, 1,000, religious, South Gate, canals, fountains, Hiram Bingham, 500, 1983

Teaching Notes

A. Crossword: Before students attempt the crossword in Activity A, have them review the vocabulary from Units 1 through 3 using the **Target Vocabulary** list on pages 145–147 where words are given with unit numbers. Then, have students use the definitions to complete the crossword. They should fill in the words they know first, using letters as clues for more challenging items. Check answers as a class.

B. Notes Completion: Have students do Activity B. Check answers as a class.

World Heritage Spotlight: Machu Picchu, Peru

Background Information

Machu Picchu is located in the Andes Mountains in Peru. The Incas built the complex around 1450, but abandoned it at the time of the Spanish Conquest a century later. It lay covered with vegetation until the Yale historian, Hiram Bingham, discovered the ruins in 1911. Nearly 100 years later, scholars still disagree about the purpose of the site. Some people believe that it was a seasonal palace for the royal family while others think it was a religious center where the Inca sun god was worshipped. Still others think it was a military fort. It may have had several functions.

The builders of Machu Picchu used cut stones to create nearly 200 buildings. The site seems to have three separate areas, tied together by a complicated water system. The sacred area is arranged so that in one building the sun shines through windows on the longest and shortest days of the year. Another area has the highest quality houses, so perhaps it was where the royalty and the religious leaders lived. The third area has more ordinary buildings, maybe for residents who worked at the site.

Machu Picchu is a UNESCO World Heritage Site and a very popular tourist destination. The environment is very fragile and landslides sometimes occur. Developers want to install a cable car, but scientists worry that this will create additional problems. A cable car would bring even more visitors and might cause more landslides.

For More Information: http://www.nationalgeographic.com/history/ancient/machu-picchu.html?fs=travel. nationalgeographic.com

Teaching Notes

Overview: The spread on pages 40 and 41 has many features. The central image is an artist's reconstruction of what Machu Picchu [pronounced **mah** chew **pea** chew] looked like 500 years ago when it was actively in use.

- The numbers in red circles are keyed to the features described in the box at the bottom of page 40.

- The yellow box in the upper left of page 40 gives basic information about Machu Picchu as a World Heritage Site. The globe shows its location in South America.
- The white box titled "The Lost City" on page 41 gives an overview of Machu Picchu.
- A glossary for unfamiliar terms is in the yellow box on page 41.

- At the bottom of page 41 is a photo of the site's discoverer, Hiram Bingham, and a quote from him.
- To the left of the Bingham's photo is a photo of how the ruins of Machu Picchu actually look today.
- The blue box above the current photo tells about a current problem with tourism.

Teaching Suggestions: First give students time to explore the features of page 40 and 41. Brainstorm what students see on these pages and make a list on the board. Ask questions to check their awareness of where information is found. Sample questions might include:
- **Where is Machu Picchu?** in Peru, South America
- **Describe where it is located.** high in the Andes Mountains
- **When was Machu Picchu built?** around 1450
- **Who built it?** the Incas
- **What is Number 5?** the Temple of the Sun

- **What is Number 6?** a canal and fountains
- **What is a *canal*?** a long, narrow, man-made stretch of water
- **Why are June through August winter months?** It is the Southern Hemisphere.
- **What is one problem Machu Picchu has today?** It has too many tourists.
- **What does Bingham's quote mean?** Nobody had any idea Machu Picchu existed.

Then, ask students to complete the field notes on page 39 as a way of extracting information from the entire spread. When individual students finish the field notes, ask pairs of students to compare their answers. If answers do not agree, ask students to show where they found the information.

Challenge: Students should explore the picture in pairs, pretending that they are visiting Machu Picchu in 1500. Taking turns, they should describe to their partner what they see as they walk through the site.

Vocabulary Building 1

Answer Key

A. Red words: organization; decision; definition; explanation; invention; permission; population; regulation; vacation; Sealand reading: **1.** population; **2.** invented; **3.** permission; **4.** definition; **5.** vacation; **6.** regulations

B. Phrases: take a trip (in title), take a break, take advantage of, take place in, take our advice, take a (camel) ride (in the caption of picture); Sentences: **1.** take a break; **2.** take a trip; **3.** take advantage of; **4.** take (someone's) advice; **5.** takes place

Teaching Notes

A. Word Link: Have students do Activity A. The suffixes *-tion*, *-sion*, and *-ation* have different spellings, but they share a pronunciation of "shun" at the end of words. Point out that sometimes the spelling of the root word changes when the suffix is added. Give students a chance to guess the spelling of the nouns before they check a dictionary. Ask for examples of each word in a sentence. Check answers as a class.

B. Word Partnership: Have students do Activity B. Remind students that word *partnerships* refer to words that are often used together with particular other words. Sometimes this is called *collocation*. In this case, the focus is on phrases that use "take" with other words as a set phrase. Students locate these word partnerships in the reading about Morocco, then use the phrases to fill the gaps in the sentences. Check answers as a class.

Unit 4 | Other Worlds

Unit Introduction

This unit discusses space exploration. Students will read about the Hubble Telescope, theories about intelligent life on other planets, the future possibility of human colonies in space, Mars, and the moon.

Key Words for Internet Research: *Alexandra Barnett, colonizing Mars, Hubble Telescope, moon, NASA, Robert Zubrin, Seth Shostak, Stephen Hawking*

For More Information: http://science.nationalgeographic.com/science/space.html

Warm Up

Answer Key

1. Answers will vary. **2.** Build background knowledge by asking what would be necessary for life on other planets (air to breathe, water, moderate temperatures). **3.** Answers will vary.

Teaching Notes

Direct students' attention to the photo and have them read the caption. Ask them:
- **What is the man in the photo doing?** walking freely in space
- **What does "walking freely" mean?** He is not tied to the spacecraft.
- **What does he need to have with him?** When astronauts walk in space, they must carry their own oxygen and the means to return to the spacecraft. McCandless II used a MMU or Manned Maneuvering Unit to move around.
- **Why do astronauts do spacewalks?** At first, it was mainly to see if spacewalks were possible. Later, astronauts fixed problems on spacecraft or collected samples when on the moon.

Lesson 4A | Making Contact

Lesson Overview

Target Vocabulary:

allow, circle, contact, distance, entire, identify, messages, powerful, search, tools

Reading Passage Summary:

Two astronomers explain why they believe intelligent life exists elsewhere in the universe and how we may soon make contact with these beings.

Answer Key

Before You Read

A. 1. galaxy; **2.** stars; **3.** astronomer; **4.** telescope; **5.** solar system; **6.** planets

B. 1. a; **2.** One reason is the amount of time since the universe started. The other main reason is the huge number of galaxies and stars.

Reading Comprehension

A. 1. b (lines 3–6); **2.** d (lines 8 and 12); **3.** b (lines 20–23); **4.** b (lines 22–24); **5.** c

B. 1. 12 billion years; **2.** huge; **3.** galaxies; **4.** smaller; **5.** radio signals

Vocabulary Practice

A. 1. powerful; **2.** messages; **3.** searching for; **4.** identify; **5.** tools

B. 1. a; **2.** a; **3.** b; **4.** b; **5.** a

Teaching Notes

Before You Read

A. Labeling: Before asking students to label the pictures, review the *hierarchy* or levels of space terms. The broadest term is *universe* that covers all of space. Within the universe, there are 100 billion *galaxies*. Each galaxy is a very large group of stars, planets, dust, and gases. Galaxies come in different shapes. Our own Milky Way, the galaxy NGC 4414 pictured at the top of page 44, and the galaxy on page 45 are all spiral shapes with most of the material in the center. Within galaxies are *solar systems*, groups of planets, and moons that revolve around one or more stars. In our solar system, there are *eight major planets* that circle the *sun*, a star that provides energy. Some of these planets have *moons* that circle them. Draw a classification chart on the board and have students label each level. Have students do Activity A. Check answers as a class.

Ask students to name the planets in our solar system and list them under *solar system*. They are Mercury, Venus, Earth, Mars, Jupiter, Saturn, Uranus, and Neptune. Pluto is no longer considered a major planet. Put an X next to planets with one or more moons (all planets have moons except Mercury and Venus).

B. Predict: Have students do Activity B. Students will need to come up with their own ideas to answer Question 2. In paragraph 2 of the reading, two major reasons are given, time and size. Check answers as a class.

Reading Comprehension

The photographs and captions on page 45 are important parts of the reading passage.

- The top caption mentions *light years*, the way distance is measured in space. A *light year* is the distance light travels in one year: 9.46 trillion km or 5.88 trillion miles. These distances are so enormous that the phrase *light year* has come to have an informal meaning that emphasizes a very great difference. *The two political candidates are light years apart in their energy plans*.
- Most powerful telescopes are located on Earth, but the Hubble Telescope is in space outside the Earth's atmosphere. Its position allows the Hubble to take very sharp photographs. These photographs have helped scientists learn about galaxies and planets they never saw before.

A. Multiple Choice: Have students do Activity A. Check answers as a class.

B. Summary: Have students do Activity B. Encourage students to complete the blanks with their own words before turning back to the reading passage. It is acceptable for students to use synonyms that have the same sense as the original words. Check answers as a class.

Challenge: For students who have completed Activities A and B, write the following question on the board. Additional comprehension questions are available on the CD-ROM.

Why do you think humans want to find life on other planets? Explain.

Vocabulary Practice

A. Completion: Have students do Activity A. You can mention that a *search* involves carefully looking for something. It often collocates as *search engine*, a computer program that looks over the entire Internet for documents that contain particular key words. Check answers as a class.

B. Words in Context: Have students do Activity B. Check answers as a class.

Challenge: For students who have completed Activities A and B, write the following question on the board. Additional vocabulary questions are available on the CD-ROM.

What two things are scientists doing to search for life on other planets?

Word Partnership

Text messaging, sending a message using a cell phone, has led to the use of *messaging* as a verb.

Throughout the meeting, Laura was messaging her boyfriend on her cell.

Lesson Overview

Target Vocabulary:

advances, benefit, independent, journey, medicine, neighbor, settlers, spread out, surface, survive

Reading Passage Summary:

The next generation of space explorers wants to establish permanent bases on the moon and possibly Mars and other Earth-like planets.

Answer Key

Before You Read

A. 1. rocket; **2.** astronauts; **3.** establish; **4.** colony
B. Answers will vary.

Reading Comprehension

A. 1. a; **2.** c (lines 7–9); **3.** d (lines 11–12); **4.** c (lines 1–6); **5.** b
B. Reasons for: **1.** living (lines 16–17); **2.** new human societies (lines 17–18); **3.** science, technology, benefit (lines 19–20); Reasons against: **1.** expensive (line 22); **2.** health problems (lines 24–26); **3.** difficult, stay indoors (27–29)

Vocabulary Practice

A. 1. settlers; **2.** survive; **3.** surface; **4.** independent; **5.** journeys
B. 1. b; **2.** a; **3.** b; **4.** b; **5.** a

Teaching Notes

Before You Read

In 2007, NASA [**naa** suh], North American universities, European universities, space agencies, and major aerospace companies joined together to support a space exploration to Mars. The program uses a robot-controlled spacecraft named Phoenix. The goals of the program are to learn about the history of water on Mars and to look for any signs of life.

In July 2008, the NASA Mars rover Phoenix confirmed that there is water in the form of ice on Mars. The discovery made some scientists optimistic about the potential for Mars to support life. However, within a few days Phoenix also found a chemical in the soil of Mars that is usually toxic or poisonous. Phoenix is equipped with a powerful microscope and camera that photographed a tiny dust particle from Mars. It really is red, so millions of tiny pieces of dust have truly given Mars its name, the Red Planet.

A. Completion: Have students complete Activity A. Check answers as a class.

B. Predict: Have students complete Activity B. They will give their opinion about sending people to live in space as a way of predicting the content of the reading. Discuss ideas as a class.

Reading Comprehension

A. Multiple Choice: Have students do Activity A. Check answers as a class. Explain that in the reading, the word *colony* means a group of people living together as they might on a permanent space station. However, *colony* also has a political meaning of a country controlled by a more powerful country. It is in this latter sense that *colonize* usually means to take over another country by force.

B. For and Against: Draw students' attention to the words in the reading passage that indicate the two positions. Examples are *advantages*, *advances*, and *benefit* for the positive side and *too expensive*, *problems*, *difficult*, and *dangerous* for the negative side. Have students do Activity B. Check answers as a class.

Challenge: For students interested in doing more with the topic, ask the following questions. Additional reading comprehension questions are available on the CD-ROM.

Would you like to live in a colony on the moon or on Mars? Why or why not?

Vocabulary Practice

A. Completion: Have students do Activity A. They must choose the correct word from the box to complete each sentence. Check answers as a class.

B. Words in Context: Have students do Activity B. Check answers as a class. Explain that *spread out* is a phrasal verb, but the verb *spread* has much the same meaning of arranging things over a surface so all of it can be seen or used easily. *Kim couldn't see his stamp collection until he spread it out all over the table.*

Challenge: For students who have completed Activities A and B, write the following question on the board. Additional vocabulary questions are available on the CD-ROM.

How is a modern-day journey to Mars similar to traveling to Australia a century ago?

Word Link

The prefixes *in-* and *im-* reverse the meaning of words they precede. For example, *dependent* means relying on someone else to survive or succeed. However, *independent* means not connected to someone else and able to manage by yourself.

Write these words on the board and ask how the prefix changes them: *ability, accurate, active, appropriate, convenient,* and *correct*. Note that the prefix *im-* is used before words starting with "m" or "p" while *il-* is used before words starting with "l" (*illegal*) and *ir-* before "r" words (*irregular*).

Explore More

Video Summary: Learn some basic information about the moon and how it influences life on Earth.

Answer Key

A. 1. debris; **2.** atmosphere; **3.** cycle
B. 1. powerful; **2.** neighbor; **3.** distance; **4.** tool;
    5. journey; **6.** message; **7.** surface; **8.** circles; **9.** entire

C. 1. The moon is about one quarter the size of Earth. It formed about 4.6 billion years ago from rock and debris from Earth.
    2. In the past, some people thought the moon was made of cheese. Others believed the moon could change people into werewolves.

Teaching Notes

A. Preview: For suggestions on building students' viewing skills, see pages 15–16. Have students look at the photo and read the caption. Ask students to complete Activity A. Brainstorm about what students know about the moon. Write students' ideas on the board and return to check them after viewing the video.

Some ideas may be:
- The moon circles around Earth once every 29 days. This results in phases of the moon such as new or crescent moon, half moon, and full moon.
- Gravity from the moon pulls tides in Earth's oceans.
- The moon has a rocky surface with many craters or holes due to hits by comets and meteors.
- Eclipses of the moon occur when Earth, the moon, and the sun are in a straight line. There are both solar and lunar eclipses.
- Humans landed on the moon in 1969.

B. Summarize: Follow these steps:
    1. Students watch the video through once, bearing in mind the answers they gave in the **Preview**.
    2. Before playing the video a second time, ask students to read the summary and fill the gaps in Activity B with vocabulary items from the box. They close their books while watching the video.
    3. After they've watched the video a second time, students complete or change their answers on the summary. Have them check answers with a partner.
    4. If necessary, play the video through a third time and then check answers as a class.

C. Think About It: Have students answer questions in Activity C in pairs. Discuss ideas as a class.

Unit 5 | City Living

Unit Introduction

This unit explores how five cities (Hyderabad, São Paulo, San Francisco, Dubai, and Venice) deal with modern challenges such as rapid growth and environmental issues.

Key Words for Internet Research: *man-made islands, Palm Jumeirah, rural–urban migration, The World islands, urban explosion, urbanization, world's most livable cities*

For more information: http://environment.nationalgeographic.com/environment/habitats/urban-sprawl.html

Warm Up

Answer Key

Possible responses are: **1.** People live in cities because they offer better health care, education, job opportunities, and chances for social mobility than rural areas do. **2.** New York, London, Hong Kong, and Tokyo are international centers of commerce, communications, and transportation; **3.** Answers will vary.

Teaching Notes

Write *Shanghai* on the board and pronounce the name [shang **high**]. Direct students' attention to the photo and have them read the caption. Ask them:

- **Where is Shanghai?** in eastern China, where the Yangtze River meets the Pacific Ocean
- **Why is Shanghai important?** It is a global center for trade and finance, and it has the world's largest port. Shanghai has a larger population than any other Chinese city.
- **What kind of buildings are in the photograph?** Shanghai is famous for its architecture, particularly the unusual designs of the skyscrapers near the Huangpu River.

Lesson 5A | Urban Explosion

Lesson Overview

Target Vocabulary:

challenges, colorful, electricity, exercise, fix, growth, property, remove, traffic, ugly

Reading Passage Summary:

Find out what Hyderabad, India, and São Paulo, Brazil, are doing to improve the lives of their residents.

Answer Key

Before You Read

A. 1. New York; **2.** 21 cities; Most of the cities will be in Asia. The three largest cities will be Tokyo, Japan (27.2 million), Dhaka, Bangladesh (22.8 million), and Mumbai, India (22.6 million); **3.** problems with housing, pollution, and crime

B. Possible answers: Have the government provide low-cost housing and better public transportation, and have city recycling programs to reduce pollution and waste.

Reading Comprehension

A. 1. a (lines 11–12); **2.** b; **3.** b (lines 15–17); **4.** d (lines 30–31); **5.** d (lines 28–29)

B. 1. Hyderabad: b, c, and e; **2.** São Paulo: a and f; **3.** Both: d

Vocabulary Practice

A. 1. colorful; **2.** grow; **3.** challenge; **4.** exercise; **5.** traffic

B. 1. a; **2.** b; **3.** a; **4.** a; **5.** b

Teaching Notes

Before You Read

A. Discussion: Have students answer the questions in Activity A. Discuss ideas as a class. The world map features a bar graph indicating the expected population of major cities by 2015. Draw students' attention to the key on the top left which indicates that the numbers in brown under the city name are in millions. For Question 2, have students work in pairs to identify the 21 cities. List columns with continent headers on the board (North America, South America, Europe, Africa, Asia) and then have students write city names under the headings. That will help them see the pattern that most huge cities will be in Asia in 2015. The 21 cities are:

- **North America:** Los Angeles, New York, Mexico City
- **South America:** Buenos Aires, São Paulo, Rio de Janeiro
- **Europe:** Istanbul (which is half in Asia too)
- **Africa:** Lagos, Cairo
- **Asia:** Karachi, Delhi, Mumbai, Kolkata, Dhaka, Beijing, Tianjin, Shanghai, Tokyo, Osaka, Manila, and Jakarta

Check that students understand the meanings of *crime*, *pollution*, *resident*, and *urban*. Ask for examples of each word. List urban problems on the board. Note that the word *issue* (in Question 3) often means *problem*. Similarly, a *challenge* can also mean a difficult situation that requires effort to solve.

B. Predict: Have students answer the questions in Activity B. Discuss ideas as a class. Check back after the reading to see if their predictions were accurate.

Reading Passage

Pronounce Hyderabad [**hai** duh ruh bad]; São Paulo [sau **pau** loo]

In British English, a *subway* means a walkway under a road or train tracks.

Reading Comprehension

A. Multiple Choice: Have students do Activity A. Check answers as a class. Question 3 encourages a broader view of the term *green* as something good for the environment. Be aware that some students may choose option "d" as a literal reading of green as "full of trees."

In Question 4, while it is true that people are moving out of São Paulo (option "c"), the real problem occurs when they drive into the city each day and cause traffic jams (option "d"). Question 5 refers to the city center, also called the *downtown area* in the reading. In many cities, this central area or inner city becomes abandoned and run-down as people move to the suburbs. Urban planners in cities like São Paulo are trying to reverse this trend.

B. Classification: Have students do Activity B. A Venn diagram is used to compare the two cities, Hyderabad and São Paulo. Check answers as a class.

Challenge: For students who have completed Activities A and B, write the following questions on the board. Additional comprehension questions are available on the CD-ROM.
1. Does your city have any of the same problems as Hyderabad and São Paulo have? Explain.
2. What is your city doing to improve the quality of life for its residents?

Vocabulary Practice

A. Completion: Have students complete Activity A. Check answers as a class.

B. Words in Context: Have students complete the sentences in Activity B. Check answers as a class.

Challenge: For students who have completed Activities A and B, write the following question on the board. Additional vocabulary questions are available on the CD-ROM.

What were some of the challenges in creating the Golden Gate Park?

Word Partnership

Traffic is a noncount noun that refers to all vehicles moving on roads in a particular area. When traffic is too heavy, *traffic jams* occur that stop the movement and cause *gridlock*, a major urban problem.

Lesson 5B   City of the Future

Lesson Overview

Target Vocabulary:

annual, construction, global, increasing, kids, particularly, shaped, successful, tourists, welcome

Reading Passage Summary:

How Dubai transformed from a small city into one of the world's fastest-growing cities.

Answer Key

Before You Read

A. 1. port; 2. merchants; 3. trade; 4. skyscrapers; 5. shopping malls

B. Dubai's population, vacationing in Dubai, building and growth in Dubai, doing business in Dubai

Reading Comprehension

A. 1. b (line 19); 2. c (lines 7–8); 3. a (lines 13–14); 4. b (line 16); 5. c (lines 31–32)

B. 1. business (line 14); 2. fastest (line 19); 3. 150 (line 25); 4. eight (lines 26–27); 5. beaches (line 17); 6. shopping (line 18)

Vocabulary Practice

A. 1. particularly; 2. successful; 3. construction; 4. shaped; 5. tourists

B. 1. welcome; 2. annual; 3. global; 4. kids; 5. increasingly

Teaching Notes

Have students look at the photos and read their captions on page 58 and 59. Ask what they already know about Dubai. Write their ideas on the board.

Before You Read

A. **Completion:** Have students use the words with definitions to complete the sentences in City Spotlight in Activity A. Check answers as a class.

B. **Predict:** Have students do Activity B. Discuss ideas as a class.

Reading Comprehension

A. **Multiple Choice:** Have students answer the questions in Activity A. Check answers as a class. For Question 3, have students refer back to the reading passage and find information about each of the options. When they have settled on option "a" as the answer, ask them to explain their choice.

For Question 5 on inference, make students aware that sometimes people say things indirectly. Choose someone to read what Mohammed Al Abbar says. He is not literally talking about being a native of Dubai. He is referring to the past and what challenges people had to meet in order to make the present situation possible.

B. **Summary:** Have students complete the summary in Activity B with words from the reading. Some paraphrasing is necessary. For example, in item 3, students must be aware that *nation* means the same thing as *country*. Item 4 refers to the ratio or 1:8 numerical relationship between native Emiratis and foreigners. Check answers as a class.

Challenge: For students interested in doing more with the topic, ask the following questions:

Has your city changed as much as Dubai in the last 50 years? Why or why not?

Vocabulary Practice

Several of the vocabulary words are adverbs or are used in their adverb form by adding -ly to the stem. Note that this has the effect of doubling the "l" on words such as *annually* and *successfully* that already end in this letter. Adverbs modify verbs or adjectives by telling how something is done. Their position in the sentence depends on whether they apply to the whole sentence or particularly to one part of it. Examples:

Increasingly, poor people are leaving the countryside for jobs in the city. (applies to entire sentence)

Hanna became increasingly upset as the carnival ride got faster. (applies especially to "upset")

Global means concerning or including the whole world. Therefore, global cities such as London, New York, Tokyo, and Hong Kong are centers of transportation and business, places with a great deal of power for the entire world.

Kids is an informal way of talking about children. People often use *kids* in speech rather than writing.

A. Matching: Have students do Activity A. Check answers as a class.

B. Completion: Have students complete the sentences in Activity B. Check answers as a class.

Challenge: For students who have completed Activities A and B, write the following questions on the board. Additional vocabulary questions are available on the CD-ROM.

1. Do many tourists visit your city? Why? Where do they come from?

2. What is a good city for tourists to visit with their kids? Why do you think so?

Word Link

Draw students' attention to the information in the **Word Link** box. Then, write words like the following on the board: *helpful, thoughtful, forgetful,* and *painful.* Have students study the word parts and then complete sentences you put on the board (e.g., *Carlos is very _____. He never remembers to bring his notebook to class.*). Invite students to make their own sentences with the words.

 # Explore More

Video Summary: Learn about the benefits and challenges of living in Venice.

Answer Key

A. 1. gondola; **2.** gondolier; **3.** canal
B. 1. Increasingly; **2.** particularly; **3.** property; **4.** kids;
   5. welcomes; **6.** annually; **7.** tourists; **8.** challenges

C. 1. Three reasons why residents are leaving Venice:
   • Property is becoming very expensive.
   • Residents have to deal with crowds of tourists everywhere.
   • Jobs are hard to find.
2. Possible answers: building low-cost housing, controlling crowds, and developing new jobs.

Teaching Notes

A. Preview: For suggestions on building students' viewing skills, see pages 15–16. Have students do Activity A. Check answers as a class.

Venice is built on a series of islands in the Adriatic Sea on Italy's northeast coast. The islands are connected by *canals,* some of which have bridges across them. However, most canals are too wide for bridges, so residents get around by boat. A *gondola* [**góne** doh lah] is a narrow, flat-bottom boat with a curved front and back. The boatman, or *gondolier,* moves the boat by pushing a long stick in the water. These boats have been used in Venice for centuries, and tourists enjoy riding in them.

B. Summarize: Follow these steps:
1. Students watch the video through once, bearing in mind the answers they gave in the **Preview**.

2. Before playing the video a second time, ask students to read the summary and fill the gaps in Activity B with vocabulary items from the box. They close their books while watching the video.

3. After they've watched the video a second time, students complete or change their answers on the summary. Have them check answers with a partner.

4. If necessary, play the video through a third time and then check answers as a class.

C. Think About It: Have students answer the questions in Activity C in pairs. Discuss ideas as a class.

Unit 6 — Clothing and Fashion

Unit Introduction

This unit explores how different kinds of clothing are used for different purposes by looking at two shoe innovators. The unit then explores the history of silk and how it is made.

Key Words for Internet Research: *chopines, Kublai Khan, M2 Trekkers, Manolo Blahnik, Marco Polo, moon boots, NASA, Neil Armstrong, Picasso, Silk Road, Vong Nguyet*

For More Information: http://ngm.nationalgeographic.com/2006/09/joy-of-shoes/newman-text/1

Warm Up
Answer Key

Possible responses are: **1.** Tom Ford, Donna Karan, Calvin Klein, Alexander McQueen, Kenzo, and Issey Miyake. Original handmade designs are known as *haute couture* and are very expensive. **2.** Answers will vary. **3.** Answers will vary.

Teaching Notes

Write the place name *Sierra Nevada* on the board and pronounce the name [see **air** ah nev **ahd** uh]. Direct students' attention to the photo and have them read the caption. Ask them:

- **What is the woman in the photo doing?** holding a silk wrap
- **What is special about the wrap?** It has a tie-dye design, and the colorful pattern comes from the cloth being tied while it is dyed.
- **What is the woman wearing?** a long dress or skirt that reaches to the ground
- **Where are the Sierra Nevada Mountains?** They are in the eastern part of California. Some of them are as high as 4,400 meters or 14,500 feet. The name Sierra Nevada means "snowy mountains" in Spanish and some snow is visible in the photo.
- **Do you know of other mountains with the same name?** in Andalucía in southern Spain

Lesson 6A — From Sandal to Space Boot

Lesson Overview

Target Vocabulary:

beyond, comfortable, costly, futuristic, heat, pair, range, rocky, stylish, weigh

Reading Passage Summary:

Two shoe innovators explain why they design shoes and what makes their creations special.

Answer Key

Before You Read

A. Students circle an example of each kind of shoe.
　1. sneaker; **2.** high heels; **3.** sandal; **4.** boot
B. The high heel was designed by a famous shoe designer. The boot is meant for astronauts to wear in space.

Reading Comprehension

A. 1. c; **2.** b (lines 8–9); **3.** b (lines 24–26); **4.** b (lines 11–12); **5.** d (lines 24–25)
B. 1. Manolo Blahnik: c and e; **2.** Dave Graziosi: a and b; **3.** Both: d

Vocabulary Practice

A. 1. costly; **2.** heat; **3.** comfortable; **4.** stylish; **5.** range
B. 1. beyond; **2.** pairs; **3.** futuristic; **4.** weigh

Teaching Notes

Before You Read

A. Matching: Have students circle the main types of footwear in the photo in Activity A. Check answers as a class.

- *Sneakers* are sport shoes with a lacing along the front opening. Running shoes are similar, but have special cushioning inside to absorb the impact of running.
- *High heels* are women's dressy shoes. The back of the shoe is very high and the heel is sometimes thin. The front or sole of the shoe is low on the ground.
- *Sandals* are light shoes to wear in warm weather so the wearer can feel cool and comfortable. They are often open on top and attached to the feet with straps.
- *Boots* come high up on the leg to just below the knee. Originally, boots were meant to protect feet from heavy work or high snow. Cowboys wear boots when they ride in a horse show called a *rodeo*. Most boots are made of leather.

When students have completed Activity A, ask them what kinds of shoes people in their classes are wearing. Why are they wearing them?

B. Predict: Have students answer the question in Activity B. Discuss ideas as a class. The high heels are very unusual because of the fur on the top. Fur is usually meant to keep feet warm, but that is clearly not the case with these dress shoes. The boot is also unusual because of the way it is made. Most boots are much thinner, not filled with yellow material and lack the metal rim on the top.

Reading Comprehension

Write the designers' names on the board and pronounce them: *Manolo Blahnik* [mah **no** lo **blah** nik] and *Dave Graziosi* [**grah** tsee **oh** see].

A. Multiple Choice: Have students answer the questions in Activity A. Check answers as a class. For Question 3, draw students' attention to lines 24–26 in the reading where the boots Armstrong wore are compared to those designed by Graziosi. The caption of the Armstrong photograph on page 66 reinforces the idea that, in 1969, space boots were so heavy that Armstrong had to leave them on the moon in order to bring back rocks.

B. Classification: Have students do Activity B. Check answers as a class. Have them support their classification in the Venn diagram by giving line numbers for their answers. Footwear that is *comfortable* feels good. Blahnik's high heels put the body in an abnormal position that makes the wearer feel uncomfortable.

Challenge: For students who have completed Activities A and B, write the following question on the board. Additional comprehension questions are available on the CD-ROM.

Do you think shoes can be a kind of art—like a Picasso painting? Explain why or why not.

Vocabulary Practice

The timeline on page 67 shows three periods in history when different kinds of shoes were in fashion or *stylish*. *Chopines* [pronounced show **peen**] were platform shoes that women wore to protect their fancy footwear from dirt in the streets. Some were half a meter high! They were *costly* or expensive, and only upper-class women could afford them. They certainly were not *comfortable*. A woman needed to have her servant walk next to her so she could keep her balance!

A. Matching: Have students do Activity A. Check answers as a class.

B. Completion: Have students complete the paragraph in Activity B. Check answers as a class.

Challenge: For students who have completed Activities A and B, write the following question on the board. Additional vocabulary questions are available on the CD-ROM.

Which vocabulary words describe most of the shoes you own? List and explain as many as you can.

Word Link

The suffix *-y* changes a noun to an adjective. Write these words on the board and have the class add the suffix: *blood*, *brain*, *hair*, *thirst*, *rock*, *salt*, and *word*. Can students use them in a sentence?

Lesson 6B — The Silk Story

Lesson Overview

Target Vocabulary:

cloth, discovery, insect, jacket, legend, nowadays, rare, unbroken, valuable, worth

Reading Passage Summary:

Follow silk across time and continents to learn about its history and some of its modern uses.

Answer Key

Before You Read

A. 1. silkworms; **2.** fiber; **3.** cocoon; **4.** weave
B. China was the first country to use silk.

Reading Comprehension

A. 1. c; **2.** d (lines 2–3); **3.** a (lines 21–22); **4.** b (lines 8–9); **5.** d (line 22)
B. Rome 3 (around 1 A.D.), China 1 (over 4,000 years ago), Mexico 5 (1522), Japan 4 (around 300), India 2 (about 1,500 B.C.)

Vocabulary Practice

A. 1. b; **2.** b; **3.** a; **4.** b
B. 1. Nowadays; **2.** rare; **3.** legends; **4.** discovery; **5.** cloth; **6.** worth

Teaching Notes

Silk is a *natural fabric* made with materials that are found in nature. Silk fiber comes from silkworms, and the fibers are spun into threads that are woven into cloth. Until the twentieth century, most clothing was made from natural materials. Nowadays, *synthetic fabric* from petroleum by-products such as nylon, acrylic, and polyester is very common and sometimes is mixed with natural fibers.

Before You Read

A. Completion: Have students complete the paragraph in Activity A. Ask them to study the photos and then use the labels to complete the paragraph. Discuss the photos together as a class. The fiber is very thin, but it helps make the point that although the actual silk fiber seems delicate, it is in fact very strong. Mention that the strength of silk has resulted in its use in parachutes and bicycle tires! Check answers as a class.

B. Predict: Have students answer the questions in Activity B. Discuss answers as a class.

Reading Comprehension

The reading passage uses the abbreviation A.D. in line 12. The tradition in Western history uses the birth of Christ as a time marker, so the years 300 and 1522 date from this point. Time before Christ's birth is marked

as B.C., meaning *before Christ*. Time after Christ's birth is sometimes given with *A.D.* that stands for the Latin words *anno Domini*, meaning "in the year of the Lord." Modern historians try to give dates in a different way—for example, *4,000 years ago*—to avoid being tied to Western culture and religion.

A. Multiple Choice: For Question 2, a *legend* is a very old, well-known story that people believe is true although it cannot be proven. While people believe a silk cocoon fell into a teacup, no one really knows if it did.

For Question 5, *actually* is used as a discourse marker to contradict something that was said or suggested earlier. It works the same way as *however* and *in fact*. In line 22, *actually* emphasizes the fact that silk is strong although it seems delicate.

B. Sequencing: Have students do Activity B. Check answers as a class.

Challenge: For students interested in doing more with the topic, ask the following questions:

Look again at the title of the reading. Do you think silk is a miracle? Why or why not?

Additional reading comprehension questions are available on the CD-ROM.

Vocabulary Practice

Nowadays is a discourse marker that contrasts the present time with the past. It signals that following information relates to the present time. Other signal words that do the same thing are *now*, *at this time*, *in the present*, or *today*. These markers typically occur at the beginning of a sentence.

A. Words in Context: Have students do Activity A. Check answers as a class.

B. Completion: Have students complete the passage in Activity B. Check answers as a class.

Challenge: For students who have completed Activities A and B, write the following questions on the board. Additional vocabulary questions are available on the CD-ROM.

1. How long did Marco Polo stay in China?
2. What valuable things did he bring home with him?

Word Link

The prefix *un-* before some words makes them have the opposite meaning. Write the following words on the board and have students tell what the prefix *un-* does to them: *broken, popular, afraid, even, educated, finished, kind, true, welcome.* In **Vocabulary Building 2** on page 76, students will have additional practice with the prefixes *un-*, *in-*, and *im-*.

Explore More

Video Summary: Find out how the people in the Vietnamese town of Vong Nguyet have made silk in the traditional way for 1,200 years.

Answer Key

A. Answers will vary.
B. 1. stylish; **2.** rarely; **3.** insect; **4.** unbroken; **5.** ranges; **6.** heat; **7.** Nowadays; **8.** cloth; **9.** jackets

C. 1. Students close their books and tell a partner about silk-making in their own words.
　2. Students might mention special costumes that people wear for holidays or festivals. Alternatively, they may mention a fabric or material from their country that is well known.

Teaching Notes

A. Preview: For suggestions on building students' viewing skills, see pages 15–16. Have students answer the question in Activity A. Ask students what they remember about silk-making from page 68. Discuss ideas as a class.

B. Summarize: Follow these steps:
　1. Students watch the video through once, bearing in mind the answers they gave in the **Preview**.
　2. Before playing the video a second time, have students read the summary and fill the gaps in Activity B with vocabulary items from the box. They close their books while watching the video.

3. After they've watched the video a second time, students complete or change their answers on the summary. Have them check answers with a partner.
4. If necessary, play the video through a third time and then check answers as a class.

C. Think About It: Have students answer the questions in Activity C in pairs. Discuss ideas as a class. An example for Question 2 is *pashmina*, a very valuable fabric made with rare cashmere wool from cashmere goats.

Review 2 | Ancient Capitals

Answer Key

A. **Across: 3.** search; **4.** survive; **6.** weigh; **7.** annual; **11.** entire; **14.** neighbor; **15.** welcome; **16.** property; **18.** remove; **19.** comfortable

Down: **1.** powerful; **2.** challenge; **3.** shape; **5.** valuable; **8.** journey; **9.** growth; **10.** beyond; **12.** tourist; **13.** ugly; **17.** rare

B. Silla, 300, Moon, Stars, seventh, Tombs, five million, 1,000, 17, rocks, Gion

Teaching Notes

A. **Crossword:** Before students attempt the crossword in Activity A, have them review the vocabulary from Units 4 through 6 using the **Target Vocabulary** list on pages 145–147 where words are given with unit numbers. Then, have students use the definitions to complete the crossword. They should fill in the words they know first, using letters as clues for more challenging items. Check answers as a class.

B. **Notes Completion:** Have students do Activity B. Check answers as a class.

World Heritage Spotlight: Gyeongju, Korea, and Kyoto, Japan

Background Information

For 1,000 years, Gyeongju [ghee **yong** joo] was the capital of the Silla Dynasty, one of Korea's ancient kingdoms. The city was well known to traders on the Silk Road and even mentioned in Arabian documents, a continent away. In 527, Buddhism became the official religion, and today tourists come to see Buddhist art and architecture. They visit ruins of temples and palaces, and see stone Buddha statues and bronze dragon heads. Many visitors go to Mount Namsan, a nearby sacred mountain. A cave in the mountain has a famous statue of the seated Buddha with three eyes.

For More Information: http://www.world-heritage-tour.org/asia/northeast-asia/korea/gyeongju/map.html

Kyoto [key **oh** toe], Japan, has many similarities to Gyeongju, Korea. Kyoto was also a capital city of Japan for more than ten centuries and is famous for its old palaces and Buddhist temples. By contrast, it also has shrines for the Shinto religion and gardens made of sand and stone. The main difference is that today Kyoto is a city with a 1.5 million population and is Japan's intellectual center with 37 colleges and universities. It is also the center of the Japanese film industry.

For More Information: http://www.pref.kyoto.jp/visitkyoto/en/theme/sites/shrines/w_heritage/ and http://whc.unesco.org/en/list/688

Teaching Notes

Overview: The spread on pages 74 and 75 has photos of important buildings in the two ancient capitals as well as lists of important places—must-see sights—to visit there. Point out some of the features of these pages before students attempt the field notes on page 73.

- The two boxes in white on pages 74 and 75 give basic information about the two cities.

- The yellow boxes on both pages tell when Gyeongju and Kyoto became World Heritage Sites.
- The globe indicates their locations in northeast Asia.
- A glossary for unfamiliar terms is in the yellow box at the bottom of page 74.
- In the lower right of page 75 is a photograph of someone tending a stone garden.

Teaching Suggestions: First, give students time to explore the features of page 74 and 75. Brainstorm what students see on these pages and make a list on the board. Ask questions to check their awareness of where information is found. Sample questions might include:

- **What countries are the cities in?** Korea and Japan
- **When did they become World Heritage Sites?** Gyeongju in 2000, Kyoto in 1994
- **What is a *dynasty*?** a series of rulers from the same family
- **Why is the tower in the left picture important?** It was built by a queen to study the night sky.
- **Why would someone visit a shrine?** to worship at a religious place
- **What is a *geisha* [gay shuh]?** a traditional Japanese entertainer who sings and dances
- **What do the poems mean?** varied interpretations, but the poets were expressing their love for their city

Then, have students check their answers to the field notes on page 73 with a partner. If answers do not agree, ask students to show where they found the information.

Challenge: Students can compare and contrast the two cities. Make three columns on the board, one for characteristics, and one for each city's name. List these characteristics and see if they are the same or different: *capital city, historical importance, large city in the past, large city today, World Heritage Site, places for visitors to see* (list *temples, tombs, gardens, special mountains, entertainment areas,* etc.).

Characteristics	Gyeongju	Kyoto
Capital city?		
Historical importance		
Large city in the past?		
Large city today?		
World Heritage Site?		
Things for visitors to see		

Vocabulary Building 2

Answer Key

A. Red words: unimportant, uncomfortable, impolite, incorrect, unsuccessful, imperfect, indirect, inexperienced, unlikely
1. uncomfortable; **2.** impolite; **3.** unsuccessful; **4.** Inexperienced; **5.** incorrect

B. Phrases: made a decision, making a lot of money, make history, make sense, made a deal; Sentences: **1.** make a lot of money; **2.** make a decision; **3.** make history; **4.** makes sense; **5.** make a deal

Teaching Notes

A. Word Link: Have students do Activity A. The prefixes *in-*, *im-*, and *un-* are all used to mean "not" and therefore reverse the meaning of words they are attached to. Give students a chance to guess the spelling of the adjectives before they check a dictionary. Note that *im-* is used before words that start in "m" or "p." Other examples that take *im-* are: *mature, mortal, partial, perfect,* and *possible.* Check answers as a class.

B. Word Partnership: Have students do Activity B. Remind students that word *partnerships* refer to words that are often used together with particular other words. Sometimes this is called *collocation.* In this case, the focus is on phrases that use "make" with other words as a set phrase. Students locate these word partnerships in the reading, and then use the phrases to fill the gaps in the sentences. Check answers as a class.

Ask students if they can think of other word partnerships with "make." Some possibilities are:

make news, make a point, make a beeline for ... (go quickly and directly), and *make up your mind.*

Unit Introduction

This unit focuses on a variety of dinosaurs and discusses possible causes for their extinction.

Key Words for Internet Research: *Carnotaurus, Chicxulub, Cretaceous Period, Dakosauraus, Deinocheirus, Epidendrosaurus, Jurassic Period, Loch Ness Monster, Masiakasaurus, ornithomimid, paleontologists, plesiosaurs, pterosaurs, Quetzalcoatlus, Sabinas, Triassic Period, Troodon, Tylosaurus, Tyrannosaurus rex*

For More Information: http://ngm.nationalgeographic.com/2007/12/bizarre-dinosaurs/updike-text/1

Warm Up

Answer Key

Possible responses are: **1.** Dinosaurs varied in size and shape and they lived on Earth millions of years ago. They are now extinct. **2.** Answers will vary. **3.** Although paleontologists have found many dinosaur fossils, questions about dinosaurs are still unanswered.

Teaching Notes

Direct students' attention to the photo and have them read the caption. Ask them:
- **What is the animal in the picture?** *Tyrannosaurus rex* [tuh **ran** uh **sor** us rex]
- **What is it doing?** eating its food, crunching a bone with its teeth
- **Is this a real *T. rex* skeleton?** According to the caption, it is a model, not a skeleton.
- **What does *prey* mean?** *Prey* are the creatures a meat-eating or *carnivorous* animal hunts for food. The animal that kills and eats other animals is a *predator*. Plant-eating animals like the prey that *T. rex* hunted are called *herbivores*.

Lesson 7A — Prehistoric Timeline

Lesson Overview

Target Vocabulary:

climate, completely, giant, hunter, in reality, museum, opposite, physically, relatives, speedy

Reading Passage Summary:

Find out whether information you learned about dinosaurs from museums and movies is fact or fiction.

Answer Key

Before You Read

A. 1. reptiles; **2.** 65 million years ago *or* at the end of the Cretaceous Period; **3.** a scientist who studies prehistoric life such as dinosaurs; **4.** meat from other animals

B. 1. no; **2.** no; **3.** no; **4.** yes

Reading Comprehension

A. 1. b (entire passage); **2.** d (lines 11–13); **3.** d (lines 21–22); **4.** a (lines 25–26); **5.** c (lines 28–30)

B. 1. T (lines 7–8); **2.** F (lines 11–13); **3.** F (line 9); **4.** F (lines 16–17); **5.** NG; **6.** T (lines 33–34)

Vocabulary Practice

A. 1. in reality; **2.** giant; **3.** completely; **4.** physically; **5.** museum

B. 1. relative; **2.** speedy; **3.** hunter; **4.** climate

Teaching Notes

Before You Read

A. Discussion: Have students read the time line and answer the questions in Activity A. Check answers as a class.

Dinosaurs existed during the Mesozoic Era, a large category of time that includes the three periods listed on the timeline:

- Triassic [try **as** ik] Period from 248 million years ago to about 206 million years ago
- Jurassic [joo **ras** ik] Period from 206 million years ago to 144 million years ago
- Cretaceous [cree **tay** shus] Period from 144 million years ago to 65 million years ago

Reptiles in the Triassic Period were somewhat different from reptiles today such as snakes, crocodiles, lizards, and turtles. Modern reptiles are cold-blooded which means they cannot produce their own body heat. Scientists believe that earlier reptiles including some dinosaurs may have been warm-blooded or able to adjust their own body temperatures. In other ways, ancient and modern reptiles are similar—they lay eggs to produce babies and they have a tough skin.

When an animal or plant becomes *extinct*, there are no more of them. Some scientists believe dinosaurs became extinct due to gradual changes in the environment. Others think that sudden changes happened because an asteroid or comet hit Earth, forming a giant hole or *crater* where it hit. The dust from the crater darkened the atmosphere so plants could not grow. The temperature also rapidly cooled down, creating a different climate. Dinosaurs lost their food supply and could not manage in a colder climate.

B. Predict: Have students read the paragraph headings and predict a "yes" or "no" answer before actually reading the text in Activity B. Check answers as a class.

Reading Comprehension

A. Multiple Choice: Have students answer the questions in Activity A. Check answers as a class.

B. True or False: Have students complete Activity B. Check answers as a class.

Challenge: For students who have completed Activities A and B, write the following questions on the board. Additional comprehension questions are available on the CD-ROM.
1. Which fact about dinosaurs was new for you?
2. Which fact was most interesting? Why?

Vocabulary Practice

A. Matching: Write *Loch Ness Monster*, *Godzilla*, *shark*, and *crocodile* on the board. Ask students to explain them or bring photos of them into class. Pronounce *plesiosaur* as [**plee** see uh sore]. Have students do Activity A. Check answers as a class.

Note the similarity between *in reality* and *actually* (Unit 6). Both signal a change from the previous material. The sentence that follows will contain facts that contradict the previous statement.

B. Completion: In Activity B, a *top predator* is a meat-eating animal at the top of the food chain. Have students complete the paragraphs in Activity B. Check answers as a class.

Challenge: For students who have completed Activities A and B, write the following question on the board. Additional vocabulary questions are available on the CD-ROM.

How are the Loch Ness Monster and a plesiosaur physically similar?

Word Link

The suffixes *-er* and *-or* can mean a person who does the action of the word root. Write the following verbs on the board and ask students to add suffixes: *farm*, *write*, *act*, and *invent*. Note that spelling sometimes changes. Can the class think of other words formed this way?

Lesson Overview

Target Vocabulary:

appearance, estimate, examine, extend, length, mystery, opinion, seek, terrible, unanswered

Reading Passage Summary:

Meet Deinocheirus [die nuh **kai** rus], one of the most puzzling dinosaurs ever discovered.

Answer Key

Before You Read

A. 1. horns; **2.** claws; **3.** unearth; **4.** fossils
B. Very long claws; an animal many times larger than a person

Reading Comprehension

A. 1. d; **2.** b (lines 6–9); **3.** c (lines 18–19); **4.** a (line 31); **5.** d (lines 27–29)
B. 1. terrible hand (line 11); **2.** in the1960s (line 6); **3.** Mongolia (line 7); **4.** arms (lines 14–15); **5.** 2.4 meters or 8 feet (lines 7–9); **6.** huge (lines 21–22); **7.** *T. rex* (lines 22–23); **8.** small (line 25); **9.** long arms (line 25); **10.** climb trees, hunt for food (lines 26–27)

Vocabulary Practice

A. 1. extended; **2.** length; **3.** sought; **4.** appearance; **5.** estimate
B. 1. b; **2.** b; **3.** a; **4.** a; **5.** b

Teaching Notes

Mongolia has an area called *Ukhaa Tolgod* that contains an usually large number and variety of dinosaur fossils. Many dinosaur eggs have also been found at this site. The baby dinosaurs inside the eggs give paleontologists a lot of information about what the entire animal looked like. The variety of dinosaurs helps scientists understand more about how these animals lived and how they interacted.

The physical appearance of dinosaurs varies extremely in body shape, size (both height and length), and in features such as horns or claws. The *limbs*—the arms and legs—indicate whether the animal walked upright on two feet or flew, like Quetzalcoatlus [ket sahl koh **aht** lus]. The length of arms, claws, and nails tells us about how the animal got food or fought with other dinosaurs.

Before You Read

A. Completion: Have students complete the paragraph in Activity A. Check answers as a class.

B. Predict: Have students look at the pictures on page 83 and answer the question in Activity B. Discuss ideas as a class. You can also ask the same question about those dinosaurs pictured on page 82 (long claws on Epidendrosaurus; horns on head and very short arms on Carnotaurus).

Reading Comprehension

A. Multiple Choice: Have students answer the questions in Activity A. Check answers as a class.

B. Completion: Have students complete the paragraph in Activity B. Check answers as a class.

Challenge: For students interested in doing more with the topic, ask the following questions:

Which explanation of Deinocheirus' small arms do you think is most likely? Why do you think so?

Additional reading comprehension questions are available on the CD-ROM.

Vocabulary Practice

To *seek* something is to look for it. The irregular past form is *sought*. The phrase *sought after* refers to something that is very rare that many people want.

When you *estimate* something, you make an approximate judgment or calculation of something based on the information you already know. *Paleontologists* estimate *that Deinocheirus must have been huge, based on the size of its arms.*

A. Completion: Have students complete the paragraphs in Activity A. Check answers as a class.

B. Words in Context: Have students do Activity B. Check answers as a class.

Challenge: For students who have completed Activities A and B, write the following questions on the board. Additional vocabulary questions are available on the CD-ROM.
1. What were pterosaurs [**ter** uh sors]? Describe their appearance.
2. How big were the giant ones?
3. Where did the smaller ones live?

Explore More

Video Summary: Near Sabinas, Mexico, recent fossil findings are helping paleontologists learn more about the dinosaurs and the climate that existed in this region millions of years ago.

Answer Key

A. 1. tail; **2.** vertebra; **3.** rib; **4.** back bone; **5.** neck
B. 1. giant; **2.** length; **3.** climate; **4.** completely;
5. seeking; **6.** examining; **7.** hunting; **8.** opinion;
9. museum

C. 1. The mayor of Sabinas probably feels very happy about the discovery of the giant dinosaur in his town. People from around the world will learn about it and perhaps visit his town.
2. Answers will vary.

Teaching Notes

A. Preview: For suggestions on building students' viewing skills, see pages 15–16. Have students label the figure in Activity A. Check answers as a class.

B. Summarize: Follow these steps:
1. Students watch the video through once, bearing in mind the answers they gave in the **Preview**.
2. Before playing the video a second time, ask students to read the summary and fill the gaps in Activity B with vocabulary items from the box. They close their books while watching the video.

3. After they've watched the video a second time, students complete or change their answers on the summary. Have them check answers with a partner.
4. If necessary, play the video through a third time and then check answers as a class.

C. Think About It: Have students answer the questions in Activity C in pairs. Discuss ideas as a class.

Unit Introduction

This unit explores the subject of fairy tales, folk tales, and legends from various countries. More specifically, the unit focuses on The Brothers Grimm and their fairy tales.

Key Words for Internet Research: *Fairy Tale Road, 4REAL, J.K. Rowling, J.R.R. Tolkien, Kalevala, medieval period, rune singers, Sleepy Hollow, The Brothers Grimm, Viena Karelia*

For More Information: http://news.nationalgeographic.com/news/2005/10/1005_051005_storytelling.html

Warm Up

Answer Key

1. Answers will vary. **2.** Answers will vary. **3.** A *legend* is a very old and popular story that may be true. It is often about a real-life hero or heroine or a famous person in history. For example, the story of how Robin Hood stole from the rich to give to the poor is a *legend*.

Teaching Notes

Direct students' attention to the photo and have them read the caption. Ask them:
- **What are the children in the photo doing?** walking in a forest in Germany
- **What is a *forest*?** a large area where trees grow close together
- **What is so special about a forest?** In Germany, especially hundreds of years ago in medieval times, people didn't go into the forest without good reason. People thought it was a wild and scary place. If children walked in the forest, they might get lost or something terrible could happen to them. Now, things are very different, and people like to walk in forests.

Lesson 8A | Collectors of Tales

Lesson Overview

Target Vocabulary:

although, appropriate, collect, magical, memorize, primarily, reflect, scary, soften, text

Reading Passage Summary:

The Grimm brothers' fairy tales are read and loved in more than 160 languages today. Learn where their stories came from and who they were originally written for.

Answer Key

Before You Read

A. These are both famous European stories about children who get lost in the forest.

B. 1. (Hanau) Germany; **2.** the early 1800s (early nineteenth century); **3.** originally for adults, later for children

Reading Comprehension

A. 1. a; **2.** c (lines 8–10); **3.** c (line 26); **4.** b (lines 29–30); **5.** d (lines 32–33)

B. 1. storytellers; **2.** similar; **3.** forest; **4.** adults; **5.** children

Vocabulary Practice

A. 1. collection; **2.** magical; **3.** scary; **4.** primarily; **5.** memorized; **6.** Although; **7.** text; **8.** reflected

B. 1. text; **2.** primarily; **3.** scary; **4.** although; **5.** appropriate; **6.** collection; **7.** reflect; **8.** memorize

Teaching Notes

Before You Read

A. Discussion: Have students look at the books and answer the questions in Activity A. Discuss ideas as a class. The main types of stories are:

- *Fairy tales* are stories for children involving magical events and imaginary creatures. The two stories on page 88 are fairy tales.
- *Myths* are well-known stories that were made up in the past to explain natural events or to justify religious beliefs or social customs.
- *Fables* are stories that teach a moral lesson. They sometimes have animals as the main characters. Fables by Aesop and LaFontaine are examples.
- *Legends* are very old and popular stories that may be true.

Ask students about famous stories from their country. As an extension, they could write, illustrate, and tell stories in a later class.

B. Predict: Have students look at the graphics and captions on page 89 and answer the questions in Activity B. Check answers as a class.

Reading Comprehension

Note that the word order of the title is for stylistic reasons. In English, the family name would normally come before the noun *brothers* as in *the Grimm brothers*.

A. Multiple Choice: Have students answer the questions in Activity A. Check answers as a class. For Question 1, it is true that paragraph 3 of the reading explains why storytelling is important in Germany (option "b"), but that is not the main point of the entire reading as option "a" is.

Note that Question 4 refers to the later fairy tales the Brothers Grimm published that did have drawings. Line 27 in the reading passage refers to earlier tales as *dark*. In this context, the meaning of dark is different from the usual opposite of *light*. In this case, *dark* means stories that were sad, unpleasant, or evil.

The key meaning of Question 5 is that fairy tales were more than entertaining stories. Each tale had a moral or message about what was right or wrong.

B. Summary: Have students do Activity B. Check answers as a class.

Challenge: For students who have completed Activities A and B, write the following questions on the board. Additional comprehension questions are available on the CD-ROM.

Do you know any of Grimm's tales? Are they interesting? Explain why or why not.

Vocabulary Practice

A. Completion: Have students complete the passage in Activity A. Check answers as a class.

Although is a marker that indicates that you are going to say two things that contrast.

Although Ingrid didn't sleep all night, she reported for duty at 6 A.M. as usual.

B. Matching: Have students do Activity B. Check answers as a class.

Challenge: For students who have completed Activities A and B, write the following question on the board. Additional vocabulary questions are available on the CD-ROM.

Will the Kalevala disappear when Jussi Houvinen dies? Explain your answer.

Word Link

The suffix *-en* changes some adjectives to verbs. Write these words on the board and have the class add the suffix: *dark*, *light*, *deep*, *tight*, and *broad*. Can students use them in a sentence to show the meaning?

Once Upon a Time

Lesson Overview

Target Vocabulary:

accidentally, affected, deeply, determined, hide, immediately, shock, suddenly, youths

Reading Passage Summary:

In the Brothers Grimm's story, *The Tale of the Seven Ravens*, a sister searches for her brothers who have been turned into ravens.

Answer Key

Before You Read

A. 1. The couple had eight children: seven sons and one daughter;
2. to get water from a well for their sister;
3. The brothers started to fight and the water jug fell into the well.
B. Answers will vary.

Reading Comprehension

A. 1. c; **2.** a (lines 5–6); **3.** d (lines 14–17); **4.** c (lines 24–25); **5.** b (lines 5–6 and 24–25)
B. a. 5; **b.** 6; **c.** 3; **d.** 1; **e.** 4; **f.** 2

Vocabulary Practice

A. 1. determined; **2.** youth; **3.** immediately; **4.** affect; **5.** deeply
B. 1. a; **2.** b; **3.** b; **4.** a; **5.** a

Teaching Notes

Many folk tales share a common structure with these parts:
- An introduction starting with "Once upon a time…" or "Long, long ago and far away, there used to be…" just as *The Tale of the Seven Ravens* does. This gives the sense that the story occurred so long ago that the exact details have been forgotten or are not important anymore. The Introduction also gives the following information:
  - The setting or where the story took place (a place near a forest with a well)
  - The main characters and how they are related (parents, seven sons, and one daughter)
  - What happens at the start of the story (the boys are sent to get water from the well)
- The Development section usually presents a problem and someone starts to work on the problem. In this case, the girl finds out she has brothers and goes to find them.
- The Climax is when the actions lead to a critical point. In this story, it is when the girl drops her ring into a cup.
- The Resolution or Conclusion is when everything works out. One of the brothers finds the ring, recognizes it, and the ravens turn into humans again.
- The Ending often is "…and they lived happily ever after." In this story the girl and her brothers all go home together.

Before You Read

A. Discussion: Have students read the paragraph and answer the questions in Activity A. Ask them about the picture of a *well* at the top of page 92. Ask students if they know of places where wells are still used. Check answers as a class.

B. Predict: Have students answer the questions in Activity B. Discuss ideas as a class.

Reading Comprehension

The Tale of the Seven Ravens is a very famous story from the Brothers Grimm. There are different interpretations of what the story means, but the most common one is that you should be careful what you wish for because it might just happen.

At http://www.nationalgeographic.com/grimm/index2.html students can read another version of the same story and listen to an audio version.

A. Multiple Choice: Have students answer the questions in Activity A. Check answers as a class.

B. Sequencing: Have students put the events in order in Activity B. When narrating a story, it is helpful to use sequence markers such as *first, second, then, next, after that,* and *finally*. Other markers used in this reading are *one day, once there, hours passed,* in time, *for years*, *eventually*, and *at that moment*. Write all the sequence markers on the board and ask students to circle them in the reading passage. Check answers as a class.

Challenge: For students interested in doing more with the topic, ask the following question:

What do you think the seven sons and daughter told their parents when they got home? Tell a partner.

Additional reading comprehension questions are available on the CD-ROM.

Vocabulary Practice

A. Completion: Have students complete the passage in Activity A. Check answers as a class.

B. Words in Context: Have students do Activity B. Check answers as a class.

Challenge: For students who have completed Activities A and B, write the following questions on the board. Additional vocabulary questions are available on the CD-ROM.
1. What happens on each *4REAL TV* show?
2. Who are the celebrities on the show?

Usage

One way to remember how *effect* and *affect* are used is to memorize phrases that show the part of speech for the two words: *He was deeply affected by his experience in helping tsunami survivors.* (verb) *The new scientific study shows a cause-and-effect relationship between a good night's sleep and performance in sports competitions.* (noun, adjective phrase)

Explore More

Video Summary: A small town in the U.S. state of New York is the setting for *The Legend of Sleepy Hollow*, the story of a man terrorized by a headless horseman.

Answer Key

A. The story is about a headless horseman who scares people.
B. 1. scary; **2.** youth; **3.** deeply; **4.** Suddenly;
    5. recognize; **6.** shocked; **7.** Although;
    8. collection
C. 1. Answers will vary. **2.** Answers will vary.

Teaching Notes

A. Preview: For suggestions on building students' viewing skills, see pages 15–16. Have students answer the questions in Activity A. Discuss ideas as a class.

The Legend of Sleepy Hollow is a short story by the American writer Washington Irving. In the story, two men compete to marry a lovely girl. As one of the men, Icabod [**Ik** ah bohd] Crane, leaves a party at the girl's house one night, he sees a headless horseman. The man fears that it is a ghost and so he leaves the town. The other man—who probably pretended to be headless—got to marry the girl.

B. Summarize: Follow these steps:
    1. Students watch the video through once, bearing in mind the answers they gave in the **Preview**.

2. Before playing the video a second time, ask students to read the summary and fill the gaps in Activity B with vocabulary items from the box. They close their books while watching the video.
3. After they've watched the video a second time, students complete or change their answers on the summary. Have them check answers with a partner.
4. If necessary, play the video through a third time and then check answers as a class.

C. Think About It: Have students answer the questions in Activity C in pairs. Discuss ideas as a class.

Unit Introduction

This unit focuses on tough and dangerous jobs such as storm chasing, fishing, smokejumping, and firefighting.

Key Words for Internet Research: *crab fishers*, *smokejumpers*, *South Dakota*, *storm chasers*, *wildfires*

For More Information: http://science.nationalgeographic.com/science/earth/earths-atmosphere/chasing-tornadoes-earth.html and http://environment.nationalgeographic.com/environment/natural-disasters/russian-smokejumpers.html

Warm Up

Answer Key

Possible responses are: **1.** Photographing a tornado **2.** Some dangerous jobs are: rescue worker, coal miner, soldiering, construction work on high buildings, explosives expert, fishing, and logging. **3.** Answers will vary.

Teaching Notes

Direct students' attention to the photo and have them read the caption. Ask them:
- **What is the storm in the picture?** a tornado, but not one with the usual funnel shape
- **What is it doing?** moving rapidly toward the man
- **Why is the car door open?** The man will get in the car and quickly drive away.
- **Why do scientists study tornadoes?** Scientists want to learn more about how tornadoes move, so they can warn people in the path of the storm.
- **Why does the man have a camera?** to compare photos of this tornado with others
- **Where is South Dakota?** The state is in the north central section of the United States, at the top of an area called *Tornado Alley*. Tornadoes occur frequently here because cold air from the Rocky Mountains mixes with warm, moist air from the Gulf of Mexico, creating ideal conditions for tornadoes in the months from March through May.

Lesson 9A | Wild Weather

Lesson Overview

Target Vocabulary:

blow, direction, frequently, occur, potential, rely on, responsible, skilled, terrifying, warn

Reading Passage Summary:

Storm chaser Tim Samaras hunts tornadoes, hoping to discover exactly what causes them to develop.

Answer Key

Before You Read

A. 1. debris; **2.** meteorologists; **3.** wind; **4.** storm
B. A tornado chaser places a device called a *turtle probe* in the path of the storm, then runs for safety.

Reading Comprehension

A. 1. a (paragraph 2); **2.** c (line 3); **3.** c (lines 11–13); **4.** d (lines 17–23); **5.** c (line 23)
B. Sequence is: 4, 7, 1, 3, 6, 2, 5

Vocabulary Practice

A. 1. occur; **2.** frequently; **3.** blow; **4.** responsible; **5.** rely on; **6.** direction; **7.** terrifying; **8.** skilled; **9.** potential
B. 1. frequently; **2.** terrifying; **3.** skilled; **4.** occurs; **5.** rely on; **6.** responsible; **7.** blows; **8.** direction; **9.** potential

Teaching Notes

Before You Read

The word *weather* in the unit title contrasts with *climate*, a vocabulary word from Unit 7A. *Climate* refers to the general or average weather conditions of a place over a long period of time. However, *weather* means the current conditions at a place including temperature, precipitation, and conditions in the atmosphere such as cloudy or clear. *The climate of the Saudi Arabia is hot and dry, but today in Jeddah, the weather is damp, cool, and cloudy.*

Meteorologists are scientists who study weather and climate. They *forecast* or predict daily weather based on information they collect from the atmosphere and from weather satellites. However, meteorologists cannot use satellite data to predict tornadoes. These storms form suddenly from a type of thunderstorm called *supercell* and then move very quickly and unpredictably. Doppler radar can "see" rain and wind in clouds, but only a short time before a tornado actually hits ground. At that point, the powerful winds suck up everything in the tornado's path, including houses and heavy trucks.

A. Matching: Direct students' attention to the world map. The yellow areas show where the *threat* or danger of tornadoes is the greatest. The colored arrows show the mix of high, cold, and dry air with moist surface air that creates ideal conditions for tornadoes. Ask students to name areas with high tornado threats. Have students do Activity A. Check answers as a class.

B. Predict: Have students answer the question in Activity B. Check answers as a class.

Reading Comprehension

A. Multiple Choice: Have students answer the questions in Activity A. Check answers as a class.

B. Sequencing: Have students do Activity B. Students put the seven events in correct order. Hint: The sixth and seventh events occur <u>after</u> the tornado and are not mentioned in the text. Check answers as a class.

Challenge: For students who have completed Activities A and B, write the following questions on the board. Additional comprehension questions are available on the CD-ROM.

Have you or anyone you know experienced severe weather? What happened?

Vocabulary Practice

A. Completion: Have students complete the passage in Activity A. Check answers as a class.

For items 2 and 3, *frequently* and *occur* can be used in either order: *frequently occur* or *occur frequently*.

Responsible can be used in both positive and negative ways. In *Greg was <u>responsible</u> for warning the town about the tornado*, he behaved in a good way by warning people about the storm. By contrast, *Hurricane Katrina was <u>responsible</u> for many deaths* is a negative use.

B. Definitions: Have students do Activity B. Check answers as a class.

Challenge: For students who have completed Activities A and B, write the following questions on the board. Additional vocabulary questions are available on the CD-ROM.

Why is crab fishing so dangerous and difficult? Why do people do it?

Word Link

The suffix *-ly* forms adverbs from adjectives. Have students use the **Target Vocabulary** on page 145 to find adverbs that can be created this way. Some words that already have the suffix are: *accidentally*, *apparently*, and *completely*. Examples of words the suffix can be added to are: *appropriate*, *bright*, *colorful*, and *comfortable*. Remember, words already ending in "l" double the letter with the suffix!

Lesson Overview

Target Vocabulary:

capable, damage, destroy, employ, equipment, height, majority, middle, occupation, race

Reading Passage Summary:

Every year, wildfires destroy millions of hectares of land worldwide. Learn what smokejumpers do to stop wildfires.

Answer Key

Before You Read

A. 1. burn; 2. hectares; 3. wildfire
B. Answers will vary.

Reading Comprehension

A. 1. b; 2. d (lines 12–13); 3. c (lines 22–23); 4. a (line 27); 5. b (lines 30–33)
B. 1. difficult; 2. spreading; 3. men, women; 4. 54–91; 5. survive/live; 6. long

Vocabulary Practice

A. 1. employed; 2. race; 3. occupation; 4. equipment; 5. capable; 6. majority
B. 1. a; 2. b; 3. b; 4. a

Teaching Notes

Wildfires can start in a natural way through lightning strikes, or they can be man-made. For example, not putting out a campfire or tossing a cigarette into a dry forest can start a fire. To stop a fire, smokejumpers must remove any fuel in the path of the fire. Sometimes they clear the trees away in *firebreaks*. At other times they start *backfires* which are intentional fires that they can control. Both of these methods use up the fuel so there is none left for the wildfire to burn.

Before You Read

A. **Matching:** Have students do Activity A. Check answers as a class.

B. **Predict:** Have students answer the question in Activity B. Check answers as a class.

Reading Comprehension

As in the photographs on pages 103 and 104, not all smokejumpers use parachutes to get from a plane to the ground. The smokejumpers in these photographs are *rappelling* or sliding down from a helicopter.

To learn more about the work of smokejumpers, visit the United States Forest Service website at http://www.fs.fed.us/fire/people/smokejumpers/ where you can also see authentic material about applying for employment. Photos featuring smokejumpers with

parachutes and recent fire pictures are available at http://www.spotfireimages.com/

A. **Multiple Choice:** Have students answer the questions in Activity A. Question 5 asks students to infer from Tishin's statement in lines 30–33 why people become smokejumpers. It is clear that Tishin is proud of his "tough guy" self-image and the excitement of jumping out of planes, dealing with the dangers of wildfires and being able to live in the forest. Check answers as a class.

B. **Completion:** Have students complete the job description in Activity B. Check answers as a class.

Challenge: For students interested in doing more with the topic, ask the following questions:

What parts of the smokejumper's work seem most dangerous? Why do you think so?

Additional reading comprehension questions are available on the CD-ROM.

Vocabulary Practice

A *volunteer* is someone who does work because he/she wants to do it, usually without receiving any money. By contrast, an *employee* is normally used to refer to a person who is paid to work for a company or organization. Some rural communities have *volunteer firemen* who work for free as community service. In the case of high school student A.J. Coston, *volunteering* means he gets training and useful experience as a firefighter. After he graduates, he may work as a paid firefighter.

Equipment, a noncount noun, describes things that are used for particular purposes in a job or activity. It never has an "s" plural form. *A smokejumper carries all of his equipment with him.*

Challenge: For students who have completed Activities A and B, write the following question on the board. Additional vocabulary questions are available on the CD-ROM.

What are some of the things that Coston has to do as part of his work as a volunteer fireman?

Word Link

Give students additional practice with the suffix *-ment* by listing the following verbs on the board: *enjoy, argue, agree, appoint, require, treat.* Ask students to make them into nouns by adding *-ment*, then use them in a sentence that shows they understand the meaning of the changed word.

Explore More

Video Summary: Follow National Geographic photographer Mark Thiessen as he chases a powerful wildfire across a desert in the United States.

Answer Key

A. good points: it's exciting, he gets interesting photographs; bad points: it is dangerous and exhausting work

B. 1. destroy; **2.** responsible; **3.** majority; **4.** races; **5.** occur; **6.** frequently; **7.** blowing; **8.** height; **9.** terrifying; **10.** occupation; **11.** skilled

C. 1. Mark Thiessen is a photographer and a firefighter. Important skills for these jobs include the ability to use a camera expertly, training in firefighting, common sense about danger.

  2. Answers will vary.

Teaching Notes

A. Preview: For suggestions on building students' viewing skills, see pages 15–16. Have students answer the question in Activity A. Discuss ideas as a class. Draw attention to the caption under **Did You Know?** on page 104. Beneficial natural wildfires have always occurred. Forest managers sometimes deliberately start *prescribed burns* to clean up forest debris. Without regular small fires, there is greater risk of a large catastrophic fire that could cause huge damage. Early in the video, there is a *prescribed burn* sign. Firefighters already know about the fire, so people don't need to report it.

B. Summarize: Follow these steps:
  1. Students watch the video through once, bearing in mind the answers they gave in the **Preview**.

  2. Before playing the video a second time, ask students to read the summary and fill the gaps in Activity B with vocabulary items from the box. They close their books while watching the video.
  3. After they've watched the video a second time, students complete or change their answers on the summary. Have them check answers with a partner.
  4. If necessary, play the video through a third time and then check answers as a class.

C. Think About It: Have students answer the questions in Activity C in pairs. Discuss ideas as a class.

Answer Key

A. Across: **1.** suddenly; **6.** examine; **7.** climate; **9.** completely; **11.** youth; **12.** immediately; **13.** appropriate; **16.** seek; **17.** occur; **18.** estimate

Down: **1.** speedy; **2.** skilled; **3.** giant; **4.** frequently; **5.** text; **7.** collection; **8.** equipment; **10.** memorize; **14.** race; **15.** warn

B. New Zealand, animals, Maori, predators, Cook, 1778, kiwi, 100, 480, kayak, helicopter

Teaching Notes

A. Crossword: Before students attempt the crossword in Activity A, have them review the vocabulary from Units 6 through 9 using the **Target Vocabulary** list on pages 145–147 where words are given with unit numbers. Then, have students use the definitions to complete the crossword. They should fill in the words they know first, using letters as clues for more challenging items. Check answers as a class.

B. Notes Completion: Have students do Activity B. Check answers as a class.

World Heritage Spotlight: Fiordland, New Zealand

Background Information

Fiordland is a national park in southwest New Zealand that the native Maori people call *Te Wahipounamu* meaning "the place of the green stone." The rivers in the area contain a special type of jade that the Maoris used to make weapons and decorations. Fiordland is a wilderness filled with snow-capped mountains, deep lakes, fiords, and other glacial landforms. It is a UNESCO World Heritage Site because it is an important *natural* area, in contrast to Machu Picchu and Gyeongju which are in the World Heritage Site list for their *cultural* importance. *Isolation*—the distance from cities and the difficulty of reaching this remote spot—has made it possible for rare plants and animals to live here and nowhere else.

For More Information: http://www.fiordland.org.nz/ and http://whc.unesco.org/en/list/551

Teaching Notes

Overview: The spread on pages 108 and 109 has a large photo of a *fiord* [fee **yord**], a long, narrow inlet of the sea with steep sides. Point out some of the features of these pages before students attempt the field notes on page 107.

- The grey box on page 108 gives basic information about Fiordland National Park.
- The yellow box at the top of page 108 tells when Fiordland National Park became a World Heritage Site.

- The globe shows its location in the South Pacific.
- A glossary for unfamiliar terms is in the yellow box on page 108.
- In the middle of the photograph is a quote from Rudyard Kipling.
- The grey box at the upper right on page 109 gives the native Maori's story about the fiords.
- The green boxes on page 109 tell about endangered birds.

Teaching Suggestions: First give students time to explore the features of page 108 and 109. Brainstorm what students see on these pages and make a list on the board. Ask questions to check their awareness of where information is found. Sample questions might include:

- **Which island of New Zealand is Fiordland on?** South
- **When did Fiordland become a World Heritage Site?** 1990
- **What does *endangered* mean?** It means in danger of dying out completely.
- **Where can you see reflections of the mountains?** on the waters of the fiord
- **Who was Rudyard Kipling? Where was he from?** a writer from Britain or England
- **What is the Maori in the picture wearing?** a kiwi feather cloak or jacket
- **If birds can't fly, how do they escape from predators?** They run quickly.

Then, have students check their answers to the field notes on page 107 with a partner. If answers do not agree, ask students to show where they found the information.

Note that *fiord* comes from the Norwegian word *fjord* that sounds just the same. The west coast of Norway is famous for its fjords.

Rudyard Kipling, an English author and poet, was actually born in India and wrote many stories set in India. His famous children's books include *The Jungle Book* and *Just So Stories*. During his life, Kipling traveled widely, visiting Africa, much of Asia, and the United States.

Challenge: If you visited Fiordlands National Park, what would you do? How would you travel around?

Vocabulary Building 3

Answer Key

A. a. advertisement; **b.** measurement; **c.** improvement; **d.** investment; **e.** payment

B. Phrases: is related to, is concerned about, are familiar with, is interested in, are (more) likely to, is committed to; Sentences: **1.** c; **2.** d; **3.** e; **4.** a; **5.** b

Teaching Notes

A. Word Link: Have students do Activity A. The suffix *-ment* changes verbs into nouns. Students read root verbs in context for meaning, then use the noun form in context in sentences. Note that the spelling sometimes changes (e.g., *payment*). Check answers as a class.

B. Word Partnership: Have students do Activity B. The combination of *be* + adjective + preposition produces a wide range of word partnerships. This exercise attunes students to some of the possibilities. Students locate these patterns in the reading, and then actively use the word partnerships in a matching exercise. Check answers as a class.

Unit 10   Pyramid Builders

Unit Introduction

This unit explores some recent information that archeologists have learned about pyramids in Mesoamerica and Egypt.

Key Words for Internet Research: *Chichén Itzá, Cleopatra, Fire Is Born, Giza pyramids, human sacrifice, Julius Caesar, Marc Antony, Maya civilization, Pyramid of the Moon, Temple of the Great Jaguar, Teotihuacán, Tikal, Waka*

For More Information: http://news.nationalgeographic.com/news/2005/10/1021_051021_tv_teotihuacan. html and http://www.nationalgeographic.com/history/ancient/giza-pyramids.html

Warm Up

Answer Key

Possible responses are: **1.** A pyramid is a three-dimensional shape with a flat base and flat triangular sides that slope upward to a point. The best-known pyramids are in Egypt, Mexico, and Guatemala. **2.** Most pyramids were built as tombs for an important leader. **3.** Answers will vary.

Teaching Notes

Direct students' attention to the photo and have them read the caption. Ask them:
- **What is the building?** It is a pyramid that was a tomb or burial place for a king.
- **Why do you think the temple was named *Great Jaguar* [*jag* yoo are]?** *Jaguars* are big cats, in the same *genus* or group as lions, tigers, and leopards. Jaguars are the only big cats in the New World. These powerful predators were symbols of strength for the royal families in Mesoamerican culture.

Lesson 10A   Ancient City: Teotihuacán

Lesson Overview

Target Vocabulary:

apparently, conclude, expert, govern, indicate, interpret, offering, official, structure, wise

Reading Passage Summary:

Mexico's Pyramid of the Moon is helping archaeologists learn more about the ancient city and culture of Teotihuacán.

Answer Key

Before You Read

A. **1.** burial; **2.** archeologists; **3.** abandon
B. They found bones of people and animals, weapons, and other objects. These may tell why people and animals were sacrificed and buried there.

Reading Comprehension

A. **1.** b; **2.** b (line 10); **3.** a (lines 14–17, 29–31); **4.** b (line 21); **5.** d (line 32)
B. **1.** T; **2.** T; **3.** F; **4.** F

Vocabulary Practice

A. **1.** structures; **2.** governed; **3.** experts; **4.** indicate; **5.** Apparently; **6.** wise
B. **1.** b; **2.** a; **3.** b; **4.** a

Teaching Notes

Before You Read

Before students start doing Activity A, pronounce Teotihuacán [tay oh tee hwah **kahn**] with them and ask them to look at the photos and captions. The photo on page 112 shows a celebration in which people dress in costumes and act out a religious ceremony like one that might have happened long ago. These performers are in the *plaza*, the flat space in front of the Pyramid of the Moon. An audience is sitting on the steps of the pyramid.

In the photo on page 113, an archeologist is uncovering human skeletons. It is unusual when the skull or head is not found, so this may indicate sacrifice. *Sacrifice* means to kill a person or animal in a special religious ceremony as an *offering* or gift to a god.

A. Matching: Have students do Activity A. Note that students had the word *tomb* in the glossary of Review 2. Point out the suffix *-ologist*, meaning someone who studies and ask for other words with this ending. Check answers as a class.

B. Predict: Have students answer the questions in Activity B. Draw attention to the map on page 113. Teotihuacán is located about 40 km (25 miles) northeast of Mexico City. It was built almost 2,000 years ago, and at its peak, it had a larger population than any other city in the world, about 200,000 residents. It has been a UNESCO World Heritage Site since 1987. Go to Arizona State University's site at http://archaeology.asu.edu/teo/ for more information. Discuss ideas as a class.

Reading Comprehension

A. Multiple Choice: Have students answer the questions in Activity A. Check answers as a class.

B. True or False: Have students do Activity B. Check answers as a class. Question 3 is an inference from the statement in line 27 that the city probably had a powerful army.

Challenge: For students who have completed Activities A and B, write the following question on the board. Additional comprehension questions are available on the CD-ROM.

Why have archeologists changed their minds about Teotihuacán being a peaceful society?

Vocabulary Practice

Pronounce Maya [**mai** yah] and Chichén Itzá [chee **chen** eet sa] before students start the reading. Maya civilization stated 3,000 years ago, and there are still Maya people living in Central America today.

A. Completion: Have students complete the passage in Activity A. Check answers as a class.

B. Words in Context: Have students do Activity B. Check answers as a class.

Challenge: For students who have completed Activities A and B, write the following questions on the board. Additional vocabulary questions are available on the CD-ROM.
1. Where was *Fire Is Born* from?
2. How did he influence Mayan culture?
3. Why is he called *wise*?

Word Link

Write a chart like this on the board to give students more practice with the suffixes *-ate* and *-ation*.

Noun	Verb
	activate
decoration	
	educate
estimation	
	indicate
investigation	
	interpret
punctuation	

Wonders of Egypt

Lesson Overview

Target Vocabulary:

according (to), blocks, compete, confirm, involve, ordinary, proud, roles, task, timeless

Reading Passage Summary:

Discover who built the pyramids at Giza, how they did it, and what life was like for these people.

Answer Key

Before You Read

A. 1. T; **2.** T; **3.** T (Answers and explanations are on page 120.)
B. c

Reading Comprehension

A. 1. a; **2.** b (lines 26–30); **3.** d (lines 20–21); **4.** c (line 27); **5.** c (line 32)
B. 1. e; **2.** d; **3.** a; **4.** b

Vocabulary Practice

A. 1. ordinary; **2.** competed; **3.** According; **4.** role; **5.** task; **6.** proud; **7.** timeless
B. 1. ordinary; **2.** task; **3.** timeless; **4.** role; **5.** confirmed; **6.** proud; **7.** compete; **8.** According

Teaching Notes

The pyramids at Giza [**gee** za] are located near Cairo, Egypt, across the Nile River. The three main pyramids are part of a *necropolis* meaning "city of the dead" because kings, called *pharaohs*, were buried there 4,500 years ago. The ancient Egyptians believed that their rulers were godlike. They believed that after death, the spirits of the kings would climb the pyramids to the sun in the sky.

Before You Read

A. True or False: Ask students about the photo with the lettered red circles. Have them locate the three pyramids, the workers' city, and their tombs. Ask them what they already know about Egyptian pyramids before they attempt the questions in Activity A. Check answers as a class.

B. Predict: Have students answer the question in Activity B. Check answers as a class.

Reading Comprehension

A. Multiple Choice: Have students answer the questions in Activity A. Check answers as a class.

B. Matching: Have students do Activity B. Note that option "c" about female workers deals only with part of the information in paragraph 3 so it is too specific as a main idea. Check answers as a class.

Challenge: For students interested in doing more with the topic, ask the following question:

In general, what was life like for the pyramid builders?

Additional reading comprehension questions are available on the CD-ROM.

Vocabulary Practice

Before completing Activity A, ask students what they know about Cleopatra [clee uh **pa** truh]. Cleopatra's story has been made popular through plays by Shakespeare and a book by George Bernard Shaw.

A. Completion: Have students complete the passage in Activity A. Check answers as a class.

B. Definitions: Have students do Activity B. Check answers as a class.

Challenge: For students who have completed Activities A and B, write the following questions on the board. Additional vocabulary questions are available on the CD-ROM.

For a time, Cleopatra was not queen of Egypt. Why? How did she become queen again?

Word Partnership

A *task* is an activity or piece of work you have to do. In a typical **Reading Explorer** lesson, students *complete* a number of *tasks* in each section. If you *take someone to task*, you criticize or scold someone for not doing their work well.

Explore More

Video Summary: Learn about the problems affecting the Giza pyramids today and what some people are doing to protect these important monuments.

Answer Key

A. Possible responses are: air pollution and too many tourists

B. 1. structure; **2.** expert; **3.** According to; **4.** compete; **5.** ordinary; **6.** timeless; **7.** proud; **8.** officials; **9.** wise; **10.** task

C. 1. Answers will vary. **2.** Answers will vary.

Teaching Notes

A. Preview: For suggestions on building students' viewing skills, see pages 15–16. Have students answer the question in Activity A. Discuss ideas as a class.

B. Summarize: Follow these steps:
1. Students watch the video through once, bearing in mind the answers they gave in the **Preview**.
2. Before playing the video a second time, ask students to read the summary and fill the gaps in Activity B with vocabulary items from the box. They close their books while watching the video.
3. After they've watched the video a second time, students complete or change their answers on the summary. Have them check answers with a partner.
4. If necessary, play the video through a third time and then check answers as a class.

C. Think About It: Have students answer the questions in Activity C in pairs. Discuss ideas as a class.

Note that UNESCO's World Heritage Site program is one way of drawing international attention to valuable natural or cultural sites that need protection. In some countries, old buildings are chosen for their historic or symbolic importance and get government preservation funds. The UNESCO World Heritage site at http://whc.unesco.org/en/list/86 has links to photos and a 360 degree tour of Giza.

Unit 11 Legends of the Sea

Unit Introduction

This unit looks at the lives of pirates from the past and in the present. Students read about which parts of the movie pirate are real and which are invented.

Key Words for Internet Research: *Blackbeard, Black Sam Bellamy, Ching Shih, Jolly Roger, Mary Read, Queen Anne's Revenge, Yucatan Peninsula, Whydah*
For More Information: http://news.nationalgeographic.com/news/2003/07/0711_030711_piratescarribean.html and http://ngm.nationalgeographic.com/2007/10/malacca-strait-pirates/pirates-text

Warm Up

Answer Key

Possible responses are: **1.** Answers will vary. **2.** Answers will vary. **3.** Old ships, weapons, coins, jewelry, clothing, plates, pottery, and so on.

Teaching Notes

Write *Yucatan Peninsula* on the board and pronounce the name [**yook** a tan]. Direct students' attention to the photo on page 121 and have them read the caption. Ask them:
- **Where is the Yucatan Peninsula?** in eastern Mexico sticking out into the Caribbean
- **What is a *peninsula*?** a piece of land that has water on three sides of it
- **What are the divers wearing?** Divers wear a wet suit for protection from the cold ocean, a mask through which air is breathed from a tank on the back, and a special vest.
- **Why are the divers using a light?** Sunlight doesn't reach very far down into the ocean. Artificial lights are necessary to see things at depth.

Lesson 11A The Real Pirates of the Caribbean

Lesson Overview

Target Vocabulary:

average, disease, divide, equality, factor, freedom, illegal, income, purchase, steal

Reading Passage Summary:

Find out what an eighteenth-century pirate's life was really like.

Answer Key

Before You Read

A. **1.** captain; **2.** maritime; **3.** goods
B. **1.** F; **2.** F; **3.** T

Reading Comprehension

A. **1.** b; **2.** d (lines 12–13); **3.** b (lines 22–23); **4.** a (lines 27–28); **5.** b (line 32)
B. **1.** Movie Pirates: a and e; **2.** Real Pirates: d, f, and g; **3.** Both: b and c

Vocabulary Practice

A. **1.** income; **2.** purchased; **3.** freedom; **4.** stole; **5.** divided; **6.** factors; **7.** average
B. **1.** purchase; **2.** divide; **3.** factor; **4.** illegal; **5.** Freedom; **6.** Income

Teaching Notes

Before You Read

A. Matching: Have students do Activity A. Check answers as a class.

During the Golden Age of Piracy in the Caribbean, the region experienced conflicts between European countries that competed for trade and political control. This was a time when slaves were brought from Africa to be sold in the Caribbean. Some slave ships were involved in the *Triangle Trade* between Europe, Africa, and the Caribbean. These ships carried valuable goods as part of the trade, so pirates were especially attracted to them.

Direct students' attention to the picture and caption on page 122. Captain Samuel Bellamy was known as *Black Sam* because of the dark color of his hair and beard. On the left in the picture stands the captain of the ship the pirates are taking over.

B. Predict: Have students do Activity B. Check answers as a class.

Reading Comprehension

A. Multiple Choice: Have students answer the questions in Activity A. Check answers as a class.

Question 3 quotes someone using ordinary or colloquial English with the phrase *They blew it.* This phrase usually means that you wasted a chance to do something important. *He could have got the role, but he blew it when he forgot his lines during the audition.* In the context of this reading, it means to waste a large amount of money by spending it quickly.

B. Classification: Have students classify information from the reading using a Venn diagram in Activity B. Check answers as a class.

Challenge: For students who have completed Activities A and B, write the following question on the board. Additional comprehension questions are available on the CD-ROM.

Is there a big difference between movie pirates and real pirates? Explain.

Vocabulary Practice

A. Completion: Have students complete the passage in Activity A. Check answers as a class.

Write *Whydah* [**why** duh], the name of a pirate ship, on the board. There have been several exhibits of the objects found on the *Whydah*. See http://www.nationalgeographic.com/mission/real-pirates/ for information about the exhibits and many links to pirate and slave ship features.

B. Definition: Have students do Activity B. Check answers as a class.

Challenge: For students who have completed Activities A and B, write the following question on the board. Additional vocabulary questions are available on the CD-ROM.

What things have we learned from the *Whydah* discovery?

Word Link

Review the prefixes *il-* and *ir-* that are used to negate the meaning of words starting with "l" and "r." Remind students that the effect is the same as *in-*, *im-*, and *un-* before words. Write the words *literate*, *legible*, and *logical* on the board and ask what happens to the meaning with the *il-* prefix added. What about *relevant*, *resistible*, and *revocable*? If students are unfamiliar with the words, have them look up both forms in a dictionary.

Lesson Overview

Target Vocabulary:

avoid, boss, fail, fearless, pretend, respected, sail, shoot, target, transfer

Reading Passage Summary:

Meet Mary Read and Ching Shih, two female pirates who ruled the waves in different parts of the world.

Answer Key

Before You Read

A. 1. a; **2.** a; **3.** a
B. 1. for adventure, power, and money; **2.** some were captured, one retired

Reading Comprehension

A. 1. a (especially lines 2–3); **2.** b (line 6); **3.** b (line 14); **4.** d (lines 14–16); **5.** a (lines 21–26)
B. Mary Read: c, e, and f; Ching Shih: a, b, and g; Both: d

Vocabulary Practice

A. 1. sail; **2.** fearless; **3.** target; **4.** pretend; **5.** avoid; **6.** shoot
B. 1. F; **2.** F; **3.** T; **4.** T

Teaching Notes

Before students start Activity A, have them look at the photos and read the captions. Ask what they already know about famous pirates. Write their ideas on the board.

Before You Read

A. Completion: Have students do Activity A. Check answers as a class.
B. Predict: Have students answer the questions in Activity B. Check answers as a class.

Reading Comprehension

A. Multiple Choice: Have students answer the questions in Activity A. Check answers as a class.

B. Classification: Have students classify information from the reading using a Venn diagram in Activity B. Check answers as a class.

Challenge: For students interested in doing more with the topic, ask the following questions:

Which woman pirate was more interesting to you? Why?

Vocabulary Practice

A. Completion: Have students complete the passage in Activity A. Check answers as a class.

Direct students' attention to the map at the top of page 129. The small map *inset* gives the larger geographical context for the main map. It shows that the Strait of Malacca is located between Malaysia and Indonesia. Each red dot on the map stands for a pirate attack between 2002 and 2007. In some places the dots are clustered together, indicating many attacks in the same place. Ask students about some of these "hot spots" for piracy. Ask why these spots are popular with pirates.

Ships in the Strait of Malacca carry valuable cargo such as oil. Because of heavy shipping traffic, they have to slow down as they travel through narrow bodies of water. This makes it easier for pirates to target or choose them for attack. The map shows many ports and islands to which the pirates can escape. In these places they sell the *stolen* goods and *transfer* them to another ship.

Challenge: For students who have completed Activities A and B, write the following questions on the board. Additional vocabulary questions are available on the CD-ROM.
1. How do modern pirates work?
2. What kinds of things do they steal?

Explore More

Video Summary: Blackbeard was one of the most famous and terrifying pirates of his time. Archeologists now think they have found one of his ships sunk in waters near the eastern coast of the United States.

Answer Key

A. 1. a cannon; **2.** They hope it is from Blackbeard's ship.

B. 1. average; **2.** fearless; **3.** sailing; **4.** shoot; **5.** boss; **6.** stole; **7.** transferred

C. 1. Answers will vary. **2.** Answers will vary.

Teaching Notes

Little is known about Blackbeard's early life. As a young man, he worked on a privateer, a ship that had the British government's permission to attack foreign ships—a kind of legal piracy. He deliberately created a terrifying image for himself, including setting his beard on fire! His reputation made ships' crews eager to give in to his demands. However, in the end, Blackbeard was killed at sea. The map on page 130 shows that he died not far from where his ship sank.

A. Preview: For suggestions on building students' viewing skills, see pages 15–16. Have students answer the questions in Activity A. Check answers as a class.

B. Summarize: Follow these steps:
1. Students watch the video through once, bearing in mind the answers they gave in the **Preview**.
2. Before playing the video a second time, ask students to read the summary and fill the gaps in Activity B with vocabulary items from the box. They close their books while watching the video.
3. After they've watched the video a second time, students complete or change their answers on the summary. Have them check answers with a partner.
4. If necessary, play the video through a third time and then check answers as a class.

C. Think About It: Have students answer the questions in Activity C in pairs. Discuss ideas as a class.

Unit Introduction

This unit explores mysteries about risk-takers who climbed the world's highest mountain, tried to be the first person to fly around the world, or sought world records in light aircraft.

Key Words for Internet Research: *Amelia Earhart, Andrew Irvine, Chihuahuan Desert, Death Valley, Edmund Hillary, Erik Weihenmeyer, George Mallory, Junko Tabei, Marfa Lights, Mount Everest, Steve Fossett, Tenzing Norgay*

For More Information: http://www.nationalgeographic.com/everest/ and http://news.nationalgeographic.com/news/2003/12/1215_031215_ameliaearhart.html

Warm Up

Answer Key

Possible responses are: **1.** The hottest place is Lut Desert, Iran, with temperatures of 70.7° C or 159.3° F. The coldest is Vostok, Antarctica at −89.2° C or −128.6° F. Mount Everest in Nepal is the world's highest place at 8,850 meters or 29,035 feet above sea level. **2.** Some people see it as a personal challenge. **3.** Answers will vary.

Teaching Notes

Direct students' attention to the photo and have them read the caption. Ask them:
- **What kind of place is shown in the photo?** a sand dune in a desert
- **Where is Death Valley?** It is in California, southeast of the Sierra Nevada mountain range—see the picture on page 63 in Unit 6. Death Valley is an ancient sea surrounded by mountains.
- **What is special about Death Valley?**
  - It is the hottest, lowest, driest place in North America.
  - It has a huge range of daily temperature from 54° C (130° F) in the daytime to below freezing at night.
  - It got its name when pioneers traveling west to the Pacific Ocean had to cross it.

Lesson 12A | On Top of the World

Lesson Overview

Target Vocabulary:

achieve, doubtful, path, previously, proceed, prove, section, significant, suffer, whatever

Reading Passage Summary:

In 1924, two British climbers vanished on Mount Everest, attempting to be the first people to reach the top. One of their bodies was found in 1999, raising the question "Did they actually reach the summit?"

Answer Key

Before You Read

A. **1.** 8,850; **2.** 4; **3.** Nepal; **4.** 1953; **5.** cold; **6.** oxygen; **7.** 200
B. Mallory and Irvine disappeared on Mount Everest.

Reading Comprehension

A. **1.** b (lines 5–6); **2.** d (lines 10, 13–14); **3.** d (line 16); **4.** a (lines 29–30); **5.** c (lines 28–30)
B. Reasons for: **1.** oxygen; **2.** body; **3.** photo; **4.** leave; Reasons against: **5.** difficult; **6.** equipment; **7.** frostbite; **8.** camp

Vocabulary Practice

A. **1.** significant; **2.** doubtful; **3.** achieved; **4.** proved; **5.** path; **6.** suffered
B. **1.** b; **2.** b; **3.** a; **4.** a

Teaching Notes

Before You Read

Mount Everest, on the border between Nepal and Tibet, was called *Mother Goddess of the World* by the *Sherpas*, the native people who live nearby. The term *Sherpa* is also used to refer to expert guides to help foreigners climb to the *summits* or tops of the Himalayan Mountains. Thus a Sherpa is not necessarily a member of the Sherpa ethnic group.

Skilled climbers agree that the greatest dangers on Mount Everest are *descent* (coming down from the top), *frostbite* (damage to your limbs when your body freezes), and *avalanches* (huge, falling sheets of snow that trap climbers). Oxygen decreases at high altitude and that affects climbers' ability to think clearly. The Mallory–Irvine and Hillary–Norgay expeditions depended on supplemental oxygen, although the tanks were heavy to carry. In 1978, climbers were able to reach the summit without additional oxygen. However, even today, most climbers use extra oxygen above 8,000 meters.

A. Completion: Have students do Activity A. Direct students' attention to the raised relief map that shows the height of the land. The advanced base camp at the bottom of the mountain is the place at a lower altitude where climbers keep their equipment and rest before starting the final climb to the summit. The red lines indicate different paths that climbers take to reach the top of Everest. Ask students to trace the route Mallory and Irvine took. Check answers as a class.

B. Predict: Have students answer the questions in Activity B. Discuss ideas as a class.

Reading Comprehension

A. Multiple Choice: Have students answer the questions in Activity A. Check answers as a class.

B. For and Against: Have students do Activity B. Check answers as a class.

Challenge: For students who have completed Activities A and B, write the following question on the board. Additional comprehension questions are available on the CD-ROM.

What surprised you in the reading about the Mallory–Irvine climb on Mount Everest? Explain.

Vocabulary Practice

A. Completion: Have students complete the paragraphs in Activity A. Check answers as a class.

Other significant ascents of Mount Everest include the youngest climber, Ming Kipa, a 15-year-old Sherpa girl, and the oldest climber, Min Bahadur Sherchan, a 76-year-old man from Nepal.

B. Words in Context: Have students do Activity B. Check answers as a class.

Challenge: For students who have completed Activities A and B, write the following question on the board. Additional vocabulary questions are available on the CD-ROM.

Why were Junko Tabei's and Eric Weihenmeyer's Everest climbs important?

Word Link

The suffix *-ever* means "any," so *whoever* means any person and *whenever* means any time. Similarly, *whatever* means "anything." *Clara's kids were free to eat <u>whatever</u> they wanted <u>whenever</u> they were hungry. <u>Whoever</u> heard of such freedom?*

Whatsoever is used to mean something generally negative. *Ken took no responsibility <u>whatsoever</u> for the accident. In fact, he remembered nothing <u>whatsoever</u> about it.*

Pioneers of the Sky

Lesson Overview

Target Vocabulary:

approach, bright, disappearance, efforts, flight, head, investigate, maintain, response, shining

Reading Passage Summary:

Over 70 years after she disappeared during a flight over the Pacific Ocean, people still wonder what happened to pilot Amelia Earhart.

Answer Key

Before You Read

A. Amelia Earhart was the first woman to fly a plane alone across the Atlantic Ocean. In 1937 she wanted to be the first woman to fly a plane around the world.

B. Answers will vary.

Reading Comprehension

A. 1. c; **2.** d (lines 3–4); **3.** b (line 5); **4.** b (line 27); **5.** a (lines 18–20, 24)

B. 1. stormy; **2.** 3,000 meters / 10,000 feet; **3.** use a lot of gas; **4.** shining in their faces; **5.** see; **6.** gets lost *or* runs out of gas

Vocabulary Practice

A. 1. disappearance; **2.** flight; **3.** headed; **4.** investigate; **5.** efforts; **6.** shining; **7.** approached; **8.** maintain; **9.** response

B. 1. investigate; **2.** flight; **3.** response; **4.** approach; **5.** shines; **6.** maintain; **7.** disappearance; **8.** effort; **9.** head

Teaching Notes

Amelia Earhart had a long flight of 4,113 km or 2,556 miles over the open waters of the Pacific Ocean ahead of her when she left New Guinea. She planned to stop at Howland Island, midway between New Guinea and Hawaii. Her target was a very small, flat island, just north of the equator. A U.S. Coast Guard ship, *Itacsa*, waited near Howland to help Earhart as she approached.

Earhart never reached Howland Island. Despite repeated efforts to find out how she vanished, investigations continue. Go to http://en.wikipedia.org/wiki/Amelia_Earhart to learn more about Earhart's life, achievements, and the theories about her disappearance.

Before You Read

A. Discussion: Have students answer the questions in Activity A. Have them read the timeline of major events in Amelia Earhart's life. Ask what other biographical events often appear in timelines (birth, early childhood, education, marriage, career points, etc). Check answers as a class.

B. Predict: Have students answer the question in Activity B. Discuss ideas as a class.

Have students look at the photos and captions on pages 136–137. What impression do they have about Earhart? Note the chain of globes on the top of page 137. Ask students to use them to tell about Earhart's attempted flight around the world. Hint: see timeline entry under May 20, 1937, for details.

Reading Comprehension

A. Multiple Choice: Have students answer the questions in Activity A. In Question 5, option "c" is an alternative theory about Earhart's disappearance, as mentioned in lines 20–22. However, lines 24 and 25 make it clear that the author of the passage favors the theory in option "a," that the plane ran out of gas and Earhart died at sea. Check answers as a class.

B. Completion: Have students complete the flow chart in Activity B. Check answers as a class.

Challenge: For students interested in doing more with the topic, ask the following question:

What is your opinion about Earhart's disappearance? Support your answer with reasons.

Additional reading comprehension questions are available on the CD-ROM.

Vocabulary Practice

On September 29, 2008, a hiker found Fossett's identification cards in the Sierra Nevada Mountains, and the crash site was discovered a few days later. On November 3, 2008, DNA test results conducted on bones recovered near the crash site confirmed his death.

A. Completion: Have students complete the passage in Activity A. Check answers as a class.

In paragraph 1 of the vocabulary reading, *despite their efforts* is a common phrase used when attempts to solve a problem fail. *Making an effort* means trying hard to accomplish something. *Despite the team's efforts, they did not reach the summit of Everest.* By contrast, something that is *effortless* is easily done or seems that way. *The Olympic gymnast made her floor routine seem effortless.*

B. Definitions: Have students do Activity B. Check answers as a class.

Challenge: For students who have completed Activities A and B, write the following question on the board. Additional vocabulary questions are available on the CD-ROM.

What are two theories about Fossett's disappearance?

Word Link

Give students additional practice with the prefix *dis-* by listing the following verbs and adjectives on the board: *agree, prove, organized, able, honest, like, obey.* Ask students to add *dis-* to them, then use the changed word in a sentence that shows they understand the meaning.

Explore More

Video Summary: A desert in west Texas is home to a mysterious phenomenon called *the Marfa Lights*. Local residents explain what they have seen and what the lights might be.

Answer Key

A. Other examples of natural phenomena include thunder, tornadoes, volcanoes, and the polar lights.

B. 1. bright; **2.** disappear; **3.** section; **4.** shine; **5.** flights; **6.** response; **7.** investigate; **8.** proof; **9.** Whatever

C. 1. It could be because the mountainous region is made up of mostly rocks containing quartz that expand during the day and contract at night due to heat. This expansion and contraction creates stress on the quartz crystals that are then converted into voltage that is accumulated over time until it is then released into the atmosphere thus creating the lights. Other people think the lights are caused by vehicle headlights.

2. Answers will vary.

Teaching Notes

A. Preview: For suggestions on building students' viewing skills, see pages 15–16. Have students answer the question in Activity A. Discuss ideas as a class.

Deserts have *mirages*, optical illusions that seem very real but aren't. For example, it is common to see "water" in a desert, only to discover that there is none there. Mirages are caused by the interaction of light with levels of hot and cold air. The Marfa Lights could be such a mirage.

A more practical explanation is that lights can be seen for long distances in deserts. A recent study by students from the University of Texas concluded that the Marfa Lights are really car headlights.

B. Summarize: Follow these steps:

1. Students watch the video through once, bearing in mind the answers they gave in the **Preview**.

2. Before playing the video a second time, ask students to read the summary and fill the gaps in Activity B with vocabulary items from the box. They close their books while watching the video.

3. After they've watched the video a second time, students complete or change their answers on the summary. Ask them to check answers with a partner.

4. If necessary, play the video through a third time and then check answers as a class.

C. Think About It: Have students answer the questions in Activity C in pairs. Discuss ideas as a class.

Answer Key

A. Across: **1.** fearless; **3.** approach; **5.** sail; **9.** income; **11.** transfer; **13.** structure; **14.** purchase; **15.** govern; **16.** factor; **17.** expert; **18.** timeless

Down: **1.** fail; **2.** significant; **3.** achieve; **4.** proceed; **6.** steal; **7.** section; **8.** interpret; **10.** doubtful; **12.** role

B. China, 1974, 2,200, Emperor, 700,000, 57, 1987, great walls, rivers, entertainers

Teaching Notes

A. Crossword: Before students attempt the crossword in Activity A, have them review the vocabulary from Units 10 through 12 using the **Target Vocabulary** list on pages 145–147 where words are given with unit numbers. Then, have students use the definitions to complete the crossword. They should fill in the words they know first, using letters as clues for more challenging items. Check answers as a class.

B. Notes Completion: Have students do Activity B. Check answers as a class.

World Heritage Spotlight: Mausoleum of the First Qin Emperor, Xi'an, China

Background Information

The Mausoleum of the First Qin Emperor is a cultural World Heritage Site because the terracotta figures give people today a window into life in China 2,200 years ago. Part of archeologists' interest lies in the figures themselves. Since each one is unique, they tell us about the diversity of the population when China became a unified country for the first time. It appears that people of many different ethnic or native groups are represented in the huge "army" of statues.

The figures also give a great deal of information about warfare in 200 B.C. including horses, chariots—carts for soldiers to ride in—and weapons. The positions of the figures tell historians that this was not a society of equality because clearly some people were more significant than others.

It is often challenging to know about the belief systems of people in the distant past. A project of this scale indicates that the Qin [chin] ruler believed that he could conquer and rule after death as he did during his lifetime when he unified China. Despite all the terracotta warriors guarding his tomb, the emperor's enemies set fire to it only a few years after he died. Although the wooden structures burned, the terracotta statues have survived in their timeless way for 22 centuries.

For More Information: http://www.nationalgeographic. com/history/ancient/first-emperor.html?fs=travel. nationalgeographic.com and http://whc.unesco.org/ pg.cfm?cid=31&id_site=441

Teaching Notes

Overview: The spread on pages 142 and 143 has a large photograph of some of the terracotta warriors. Point out these features of these pages before students attempt the field notes on page 141.

- The left white box on page 142 gives basic information about the discovery of the warriors.

- The yellow box on page 142 tells when the Mausoleum became a World Heritage Site.
- The globe shows its location in central China.
- A glossary for unfamiliar terms is in the yellow box on page 143.
- The red boxes on page 143 tell about the emperor, his tomb, and some figures who are not warriors.

Teaching Suggestions: First give students time to explore the features of page 142 and 143. Brainstorm what students see on these pages and make a list on the board. Ask questions to check their awareness of where information is found. Sample questions might include:

- **Where are the terracotta statues?** in Shaanxi [shan **she**] Province in central China
- **When did the *Mausoleum* become a World Heritage Site?** 1987
- **What is a *mausoleum*?** a place for a tomb
- **Who found the statues?** local farmers
- **How many statues are there?** more than 7,000
- **Were the statues always the same color of brown?** No, they were brightly colored.
- **What was Emperor Qin Shihuang famous for?** He was the first emperor of unified China.
- **Why haven't archeologists opened the emperor's tomb yet?** They are worried that light and air will damage it.

Then, ask students to check their answers to the field notes on page 141 with a partner. If answers do not agree, ask students to show where they found the information.

Terracotta, a red clay, was commonly used for pottery in the area near Xi'an. The clay came from a nearby mountain. Skilled workers used an assembly line process to shape the bodies and limbs of the clay warriors, and then made changes in the faces so that each individual looked different.

Emperor Qin Shihuang took many steps to keep the newly unified China together. These included building a great wall to keep out enemies from the north, creating a legal system, developing standard ways of measuring height and weight, and building a nationwide system of roads. Despite these positive steps, he is noted for restricting the freedom of scholars and people who disagreed with him.

The emperor was afraid of death. A historian of that time said that the emperor drank *mercury*—a poison—because he thought it would make him live forever. Instead, it caused his death.

Challenge: What do you think the farmers who found the warriors thought? Explain.

Vocabulary Building 4

Answer Key

A. 1. careful; **2.** painless; **3.** hopeful; **4.** peaceful; **5.** senseless; **6.** heartless; **7.** thankful
Word Link usage: **1.** peace; **2.** sense, heart

B. Phrases: vanished into, escaped from, traveled to, disagree with, responded to; Sentences: **1.** escaped from; **2.** disagree with; **3.** travel to

Teaching Notes

A. Word Link: Have students do Activity A. The suffixes *-ful* and *-less* change nouns into adjectives. Students read the paragraphs and fill the gaps with the appropriate suffix. Check answers as a class.

B. Word Partnership: Have students do Activity B. Some nouns—like *care* and *hope*—can be used with both suffixes. However, other nouns can take only one of the suffixes. For example, a situation can be *peaceful*, but not *peaceless* in English. There is no such word as *heartful* but a close relative in meaning is *heartfelt*. *Suzy had her friends' heartfelt wishes as she recovered from her illness.* Check answers as a class.

Target Vocabulary Definitions

Word	Definition
abroad	(adv.) overseas, in a foreign country
accidentally	(adv.) unintentionally; happening by chance, not on purpose
according (to)	(phrase) as stated by or in agreement with a particular source
achieve	(v.) to succeed in doing something after a lot of effort
advance	(n.) progress in a particular field
advantage	(n.) a way in which one thing is better than another
advice	(n.) an opinion about what someone should do in a particular situation
affect	(v.) to influence or change a person, thing, or situation
alike	(adj.) similar
allow	(v.) to give permission to do something or not to do anything to prevent it
although	(conj.) used to introduce a contrasting statement
ancient	(adj.) very old, having existed for a long time
annual	(adj.) happening once a year
apparently	(adv.) used to refer to something that seems to be true, but you're not sure if it is or not
appearance	(n.) the way someone or something looks
approach	(v.) to get closer to something
appropriate	(adj.) suitable or acceptable for a situation
artist	(n.) someone who draws, paints, or produces works of art, or a person who performs such as a musician or actor
assist	(v.) to help someone
attitude	(n.) the way one thinks and feels about something
audience	(n.) a group of people who watch or listen to a play, concert, movie, television program, and so on
average	(adj.) normal or ordinary
avoid	(v.) to prevent something from happening or keep away from something

Word	Definition
background	(n.) the kind of family one comes from and the kind of education one has
baggage	(n.) bags that you take with you when you travel
belong (to)	(v.) to be the property of a person or thing
benefit	(v.) to help or improve your life in some way
beyond	(prep.) on the other side of a place
block	(n.) a large rectangular or square piece of stone
blow	(v.) to move with speed or force
boss	(n.) the person in charge of an organization or other workers
bright	(adj.) shining strongly, full of light
capable	(adj.) able to do something
century	(n.) a period of 100 years
challenge	(n.) something new and difficult that requires great effort and determination
circle	(v.) to move around something in a circle
climate	(n.) the general weather conditions that are typical of a place
cloth	(n.) fabric made by knitting or weaving a substance like cotton or wool
club	(n.) a place, like a nightclub, where people go for entertainment
collection	(n.) a group of similar or related things
colorful	(adj.) something with bright or striking colors or a lot of colors; interesting and exciting
comfortable	(adj.) making a person feel relaxed; providing a good feeling
compete	(v.) to take part in a contest or a game and try to win
completely	(adv.) totally, entirely
conclude	(v.) to decide that something is true, given the facts that you know about it
confirm	(v.) to say that something you thought was true is definitely true
construction	(n.) the building or creating of something
contact	(v.) to send a message to someone
conversation	(n.) a talk with someone, usually in an informal situation

costly	(adj.) very expensive
creative	(adj.) able to invent, create, and develop original ideas
damage	(v.) to break or harm something
deeply	(adv.) strongly, seriously
despite	(prep.) even though; used to introduce a fact that makes something surprising
destroy	(v.) to cause so much damage that something is completely ruined
determined	(adj.) having made a firm decision to do something despite opposition
differ	(v.) to be unlike something else, to disagree
direction	(n.) a line leading to a place or point
disappearance	(n.) an act of vanishing; going to a place that cannot be found
discovery	(n.) awareness of something that was not known before, finding something for the first time
disease	(n.) an illness that affects people, animals, or plants
distance	(n.) the degree or amount of space between two places
divide	(v.) to separate into smaller groups or parts
doubtful	(adj.) unlikely or uncertain
earn	(v.) to receive money in return for work that one does
effort	(n.) an attempt; trying and working very hard to do something
electricity	(n.) a form of energy used for heating, lighting, and running machines
employ	(v.) to give someone a job to do for payment
encourage	(v.) to give someone confidence, letting the person know what they are doing is good
entire	(adj.) the whole of (something)
equality	(n.) the same status, rights, advantages, and responsibilities for everyone
equipment	(n.) things that are used for a particular purpose such as a job or hobby
escape	(v.) to succeed in getting away from someone, something, or some place
especially	(adv.) applying more to one person, things, and so on than to any others; in particular
estimate	(n.) an approximate judgment or calculation

eventually	(adv.) in the end
examine	(v.) to look at someone or something very carefully
exercise	(v.) to move your body energetically to get in shape and remain healthy
expert	(n.) a person who is very skilled at something or knowledgeable about it
extend	(v.) to stretch or spread (something) out to greater or fullest length
extreme	(adj.) very great in degree or intensity
face	(v.) to deal with something that is difficult or unpleasant
factor	(n.) one of the things that affects an event, decision, or situation
fail	(v.) to not succeed in doing something
familiar	(adj.) used to describe someone or something that you recognize and know well
fearless	(adj.) not afraid at all
female	(adj.) referring to women and girls
fill	(v.) to take up an area so that it is full, to use all available space
fix	(v.) to repair something that is damaged or not working properly
flight	(n.) a trip made by or in an airplane
form	(v.) to develop or start something
freedom	(n.) the state of being allowed to do what one wants to do
frequently	(adv.) often
futuristic	(adj.) something that looks or seems very modern and unusual
gentle	(adj.) kind, mild, and calm
giant	(adj.) huge, much larger than others of its kind
global	(adj.) including the whole world
goal	(n.) something to achieve, although it will take much time and effort
govern	(v.) to officially rule a city or country
growth	(n.) development in size, wealth, or importance
head	(v.) to move in a certain direction
heat	(n.) warmth or the quality of being hot
heavily	(adv.) strongly
height	(n.) the size or length of something from top to bottom
hide	(v.) to put something or someone in a place where they cannot easily be found

hit	(v.) to be touched or struck with a lot of force
huge	(adj.) something extremely large in size, amount, or degree
hunter	(n.) a person or animal that searches for other animals to kill for food
identify	(v.) to discover or notice the existence of something
illegal	(adj.) something the law says is not allowed
immediately	(adv.) without delay, right away
income	(n.) money earned or received
increasingly	(adv.) becoming greater in intensity or more common
independent	(adj.) separate, not connected to or influenced by others
indicate	(v.) to show what or where something is
influence	(v.) to have an effect on something
insect	(n.) a very small animal that has six legs and usually wings
intelligent	(adj.) having the ability to think, understand, and learn things quickly and well
interpret	(v.) to decide on the meaning of something that is not clear
invent	(v.) to create something new that did not exist before
investigate	(v.) to try to find out what happened or what the truth is
involve	(v.) to take part or participate in a situation, event, or activity
issue	(n.) a subject that people argue about or discuss
jacket	(n.) a short coat with long sleeves
journey	(n.) travel from one place to another
kid	(n.) a child (informal use)
legend	(n.) a very old and popular story that may be true
length	(n.) the size or measurement of something from one end to the other
lively	(adj.) quick and full of energy, cheerful
magical	(adj.) wonderful or mysterious
maintain	(v.) to keep something going in good condition, level, or standard
majority	(n.) the largest part of a group of people or thing

medicine	(n.) the treatment of illness and injuries by doctors and nurses
memorize	(v.) to learn something so one can remember it exactly
message	(n.) information that someone is trying to communicate
method	(n.) a particular way of doing something
middle	(n.) the part of something that is furthest from its edges; the center
mix	(n.) two or more different things together
museum	(n.) a building where a large number of interesting and valuable things are kept
mystery	(n.) something that is not known or understood
native	(n.) someone born in a particular place
neighbor	(n.) someone who lives near or next to you
nowadays	(adv.) at the present time, in contrast with the past
occupation	(n.) a job or profession
occur	(v.) happen
offering	(n.) a religious gift
official	(n.) a government authority
opinion	(n.) a personal belief or view
opposite	(n.) a totally different thing or opinion
ordinary	(adj.) normal; not special or different in any way
organization	(n.) a group of people with a common purpose
pair	(n.) two things of the same, or similar, type
particularly	(adv.) especially
path	(n.) a strip of ground that people walk on
peace	(n.) a state of quiet and calm; not war
performance	(n.) entertaining an audience by singing, dancing, or acting
physically	(adv.) in or of the body
polite	(adj.) having or showing good manners
popular	(adj.) well liked by a lot of people
population	(n.) all the people who live in a particular area, city, or country
potential	(n.) the possibility for doing something

powerful	(adj.) very strong or effective
pretend	(v.) to make believe something is true
previous	(adj.) happening or existing before something that follows
primarily	(adv.) mainly, first of all
proceed	(v.) to continue, to carry on doing something
properly	(adv.) correctly, in a satisfactory way
property	(n.) a building and the land around it; also, all the things that belong to someone
proud	(adj.) pleased and satisfied about something good you've done
prove	(v.) to show that something is true
purchase	(v.) to buy something
race	(v.) to go very quickly
range	(v.) to vary on a scale of measurement, price, or quality
rare	(adj.) something that is not common and therefore valuable
(in) reality	(phrase) used to introduce a statement about the real nature of something; actually, in fact
recognize	(v.) to recall or remember something when you see or hear a person or thing
reflect	(v.) to mirror or give a true idea about something
region	(n.) an area of a country or the world
relative	(n.) a member of your family
relax	(v.) to feel more calm and less tense
religious	(adj.) connected with religion
rely (on)	(v.) to need or depend on someone or something in order to live or work properly
remove	(v.) to take something away
respected	(adj.) admired or considered important by many people
response	(n.) a reply or reaction
responsible	(adj.) being the cause of something
rocky	(adj.) covered with rocks
role	(n.) a position or function in a situation
sail	(v.) to travel by boat over the seas
scary	(adj.) something that is frightening
search (for)	(v.) to look carefully for something
section	(n.) a part of something
seek	(v.) to try to find or obtain something
settler	(n.) a person who goes to live in a new country or place

shaped	(adj.) something that has the shape of another object or is formed in a particular way
shine	(v.) to produce or reflect light
shock	(v.) to be very upset because of something unpleasant you didn't expect
shoot	(v.) to kill or injure someone by firing a bullet or by using an arrow
significant	(adj.) important or noticeable
skilled	(adj.) having the knowledge and ability to do something well
smart	(adj.) clever or intelligent
soften	(v.) to make something milder or less severe
specific	(adj.) precise and exact
speedy	(adj.) fast
spread (out)	(v.) to reach or extend to a larger area
steal	(v.) to take something without permission and without intending to return it
strategy	(n.) a plan to achieve something, especially over a long period
strength	(n.) the physical energy to perform various actions
structure	(n.) something built from parts connected in an ordered way
stylish	(adj.) elegant and fashionable
successful	(adj.) having achieved a desired result
suddenly	(adv.) quickly and unexpectedly
suffer	(v.) to be badly affected by a disease, pain, sadness, a lack of something, etc
surface	(n.) the outside or flat top part of something
survive	(v.) to live through a dangerous situation
system	(n.) a way of doing something that follows a fixed plan or set of rules
target	(v.) to decide to attack a particular person, thing, or place
task	(n.) an activity or piece of work that one has to do
terrible	(adj.) extremely bad
terrifying	(adj.) extremely frightening
text	(n.) written material
tie	(v.) to fasten things together with a knot

timeless	(*adj.*) used to describe something that is so good or beautiful that it is not affected by changes in society or fashion
tool	(*n.*) an instrument or piece of equipment
tourist	(*n.*) a person who travels for pleasure
traffic	(*n.*) all the vehicles moving along roads in a particular area
trainer	(*n.*) someone who teaches people or animals necessary skills
transfer	(*v.*) to change from one place or situation to another
trip	(*n.*) a journey to a particular place
ugly	(*adj.*) unattractive and unpleasant to look at
unanswered	(*adj.*) not answered or replied to
unbroken	(*adj.*) continuous and complete
valuable	(*adj.*) useful, helpful, or worth a lot of money
warn	(*v.*) to tell someone about a possible danger or problem
weigh	(*v.*) to measure how heavy someone or something is
welcome	(*v.*) to approve of an action or decision; also to greet in a friendly way
whatever	(*conj.*) used to indicate something that is not precisely known
wise	(*adj.*) experienced, knowledgeable, and sensible in making decisions
worth	(*adj.*) equal in value to something
youth	(*n.*) a young person, especially a young man

Glossary of Terms

Term	Definition
affix	letters added to the beginning (prefix) or end (suffix) of a word that change the word's meaning and part of speech
caption	a title or description printed underneath or next to a photograph or other graphic
chunking	reading text in groups of words such as phrases, not reading word by word
cloze	a technique for checking comprehension of a text by omitting words from a passage and substituting gaps
collocation	words that frequently occur together, for example, "blonde hair"
extensive reading	reading longer texts outside the classroom, primarily for interest or pleasure, at a language level that is appropriate for the reader
gist comprehension	understanding the general meaning or sense of a text
graphic organizer	a visual way of showing the relationship of ideas from a text. Examples used in *Reading Explorer* are timelines, Venn diagrams, and word webs.
high-frequency vocabulary	the most commonly occurring and useful words that students need to know for reading
inference	understanding meaning that is not directly stated in a text; "reading between the lines"
intensive reading	guided, detailed reading often done in class for a particular purpose, such as building vocabulary or developing reading skills
linear text	prose or written text, as contrasted to graphically presented material such as photographs, videos, maps, and charts
main idea	the most important idea of a paragraph or entire reading passage
mnemonic	a memory aid, such as associating a word with a picture, to make something easier to learn or remember
paraphrasing	expressing the same idea using different words
reference	the relationship between a word—for example, a pronoun such as *it* and *him*—which stands for another name, word, or idea mentioned elsewhere in the reading passage
scan	to read quickly in search of specific information, such as names and dates
skim	to read quickly to determine the gist of a passage or the main ideas
subvocalizing	pronouncing words quietly while reading; moving lips, tongue, and throat
summary	a short account of a reading or video that gives only the main ideas
timeline	a graphic organizer that shows the relationship between events in chronological order. For example, see page 78 of Student Book 1.
Venn diagram	a type of graphic organizer with two or more overlapping circles that indicate comparison (where things are the same) and contrast (where things are different). For example, see page 12 of Student Book 1.
visual literacy	understanding and interpreting information in the form of photographs, videos, maps, and graphic images such as charts and diagrams; also referred to as "graphic literacy."
word map	a graphic organizer that shows how words and ideas are related to each other. For example, see page 36 of Student Book 1.

Recommended Graded Readers

The *Footprint Reading Library* is a nonfiction series of graded readers that presents fascinating real-life stories in three formats: print, audio, and video. The series uses material from National Geographic Digital Media and is an ideal accompaniment to *Reading Explorer*, particularly for after-class extensive reading practice.

Each of the units in *Reading Explorer 1* is tied—thematically and in terms of approximate language level—to one of the *Footprint Reading Library* titles; see the following table.

For more information on the *Footprint Reading Library*, visit elt.heinle.com/ng

Unit	Theme	Recommended Footprint title
1	Amazing Animals	Monkey Party
2	Travel and Adventure	Volcano Trek
3	Music and Festivals	Taiko Master*
Review 1	City in the Clouds	Lost City of Machu Picchu
4	Other Worlds	Columbus and the New World
5	City Living	A Special Kind of Neighborhood*
6	Clothing and Fashion	Peruvian Weaver*
Review 2	Ancient Capitals	Last of the Cheju Divers*
7	Dinosaurs Come Alive	Dinosaur Search*
8	Stories and Storytellers	Dreamtime Painters
9	Tough Jobs	Making a Thai Boxing Champion*
Review 3	Land of Legends	Water Sports Adventure*
10	Pyramid Builders	The Giant's Causeway
11	Legends of the Sea	Life on the Orinoco
12	Vanished!	Alaskan Ice Climbing
Review 4	The Hidden Warriors	Young Riders of Mongolia
Titles marked * are at 1000 headwords level; other titles are at 800 headwords level.		